THE
FIRST HUNDRED THOUSAND

IAN HAY

RICHARD DREW PUBLISHING LTD

Glasgow

First published 1915
by William Blackwood & Sons

This edition first published 1985
by Richard Drew Publishing Ltd
6 Clairmont Gardens, Glasgow G3 7LW, Scotland

British Library Cataloguing in Publication data
Hay, Ian
The first hundred thousand.
I. Title
823′.912[F]   PR6003.E42

ISBN 0-86267-137-X
ISBN 0-86267-136-1 Pbk

Printed in Great Britain by
Blantyre Printing & Binding Co Ltd

BOOK ONE

BLANK CARTRIDGES

"K(1)."

We do not deem ourselves A 1,
We have no past: we cut no dash:
Nor hope, when launched against the Hun,
To raise a more than moderate splash.

But yesterday, we said farewell
To plough; to pit; to dock; to mill.
For glory? Drop it! Why? Oh well—
To have a slap at Kaiser Bill.

And now today has come along.
With rifle, haversack, and pack,
We're off, a hundred thousand strong.
And — some of us will not come back.

But all we ask, if that befall,
Is this. Within your hearts be writ
This single line memorial:—
He did his duty — and his bit!

CHAPTER ONE

AB OVO

"Squoad – '*shun!* Move to the right in fours. Forrm — *fourrs!*"

The audience addressed looks up with languid curiosity, but makes no attempt to comply with the speaker's request.

"Come away now, come away!" urges the instructor, mopping his brow. "Mind me: on the command 'form fours', odd numbers will stand fast; even numbers tak' a shairp pace to the rear and anither to the right. Now — forrm *fourrs!*"

The squad stands fast, to a man. Apparently — nay, verily — they are all odd numbers.

The instructor addresses a gentlemen in a decayed Homburg hat, who is chewing tobacco in the front rank.

"Yous, what's your number?"

The ruminant ponders.

"Seeven fower ought seeven seeven," he announces, after a prolonged mental effort.

The instructor raises clenched hands to heaven.

"Man, I'm no' askin' you your regimental number! Never heed that. It's your number in the squad I'm seeking. You numbered off frae the right five minutes syne."

Ultimately it transpires that the culprit's number is

ten. He is pushed into his place, in company with the other even numbers, and the squad finds itself approximately in fours.

"Forrm — two *deep!*" barks the instructor.

The fours disentangle themselves reluctantly, Number Ten being the last to forsake his post.

"Now we'll dae it just yince more, and have it right," announces the instructor, with quite unjustifiable optimism. "Forrm — *fourrs!*"

This time the result is better, but there is confusion on the left flank.

"Yon man, oot there on the left," shouts the instructor, "what's your number?"

Private Mucklewame, whose mind is slow but tenacious, answers — not without pride at knowing —

"Nineteen!"

(Thank goodness, he reflects, odd numbers stand fast upon all occasions.)

"Weel, mind this," says the sergeant — "Left files is always even numbers, even though they are odd numbers."

This revelation naturally clouds Private Mucklewame's intellect for the afternoon; and he wonders dimly, not for the first time, why he ever abandoned his well-paid and well-fed job as a butcher's assistant in distant Wishaw ten long days ago.

And so the drill goes on. All over the drab, dusty, gritty parade-ground, under the warm September sun, similar squads are being pounded into shape. They have no uniforms yet: even their instructors wear bowler hats or cloth caps. Some of the faces under the brims of these hats are not too prosperous. The junior officers are drilling squads too. They are a little shaky in what an actor would call their "patter", and they are inclined to lay stress on the wrong syllables; but they move their squads about somehow. Their seniors are dotted about the square, vigilant and helpful — here prompting a rusty sergeant instructor, there unravelling a squad which, in a spirited but misguided endeavour to obey an impossible order from Second Lieutenant Bobby Little, has wound itself up into a formation closely resembling the third figure of the Lancers.

Over there, by the officers' mess, stands the Colonel. He is in uniform, with a streak of parti-coloured ribbon running across above his left-hand breast-pocket. He is pleased to call himself a "dug-out". A fortnight ago he was fishing in the Garry, his fighting days avowedly behind him, and only the Special Reserve between him and *embonpoint*. Now he finds himself pitchforked back into the Active List, at the head of a battalion eleven hundred strong.

He surveys the scene. Well, his officers are all right. The Second in Command has seen almost as much service as himself. Of the four company commanders, two have been commandeered while home on leave from India, and the other two have practised the art of war in company with brother Boer. Of the rest, there are three subalterns from the Second Battalion — left behind, to their unspeakable woe — and four from the O.T.C. The juniors are very junior, but keen as mustard.

But the men! Is it possible? Can that awkward, shy, self-conscious mob, with scarcely an old soldier in their ranks, be pounded, within the space of a few months, into the Seventh (Service) Battalion of the Bruce and Wallace Highlanders — one of the most famous regiments in the British Army?

The Colonel's boyish figure stiffens.

"They're a rough crowd," he murmurs, "and a tough crowd: but they're a stout crowd. By gad! We'll make them a credit to the Old Regiment yet!"

CHAPTER TWO

THE DAILY GRIND

WE HAVE BEEN in existence for more than three weeks now, and occasionally we are conscious of a throb of real life. Squad drill is almost a thing of the past, and we work by platoons of over fifty men. Today our platoon once marched, in perfect step, for seven complete and giddy paces, before disintegrating into its usual formation — namely, an advance in irregular *échelon,* by individuals.

Four platoons form a company, and each platoon is (or should be) led by a subaltern, acting under his company commander. But we are very short of subalterns at present. (We are equally short of N.C.O.'s; but then you can always take a man out of the ranks and christen him sergeant, whereas there is no available source of Second Lieutenants save capricious Whitehall.) Consequently, three platoons out of four in our company are at present commanded by N.C.O.'s, two of whom appear to have retired from active service about the time that bows and arrows began to yield place to the arquebus, while the third has been picked out of the ranks simply because he possesses a loud voice and a cake of soap. None of them has yet mastered the new drill — it was all changed at the beginning of this year — and the majority of the officers are in no position to correct their anachronisms.

Still, we are getting on. Number Three Platoon

(which boasts a subaltern) has just marched right round the barrack square, without—

(1) Marching through another platoon.

(2) Losing any part or parts of itself.

(3) Adopting a formation which brings it face to face with a blank wall, or piles it up in a tidal wave upon the verandah of the married quarters.

They could not have done that a week ago.

But stay, what is this disturbance on the extreme left? The command "Right form" has been given, but six files on the outside flank have ignored the suggestion, and are now advancing (in skirmishing order) straight for the ashbin outside the cookhouse door, looking piteously round over their shoulders for some responsible person to give them an order which will turn them about and bring them back to the fold. Finally they are rounded up by the platoon sergeant, and restored to the strength.

"What went wrong, Sergeant?" inquires Second Lieutenant Bobby Little. He is a fresh-faced youth, with an engaging smile. Three months ago he was keeping wicket for his school eleven.

The sergeant comes briskly to attention.

"The order was not distinctly heard by the men, sir," he explains, "owing to the corporal that passed it on wanting a tooth. Corporal Blain, three paces forward — march!"

Corporal Blain steps forward, and after remembering to slap the small of his butt with his right hand, takes up his parable—

"I was sittin' doon tae ma dinner on Sabbath, sir, when my front teeth met upon a small piece of bone that was stickit in —"

Further details of this gastronomic tragedy are cut short by the blast of a whistle. The Colonel, at the other side of the square, has given the signal for the end of parade. Simultaneously a bugle rings out cheerfully from the direction of the orderly-room. Breakfast, blessed breakfast, is in sight. It is nearly eight, and we have been as busy as bees since six.

At a quarter to nine the battalion parades for a route march. This, strange as it may appear, is a comparative rest. Once you have got your company safely decanted from column of platoons into column of route, your labours are at an end. All you have to do is to march; and that is no great hardship when you are as hard as nails, as we are fast becoming. On the march the mental gymnastics involved by the formation of an advanced guard or the disposition of a piquet line are removed to a safe distance. There is no need to wonder guiltily whether you have sent out a connecting-file between the vanguard and the main-guard, or if you remember to instruct your sentry groups as to the position of the enemy and the extent of their own front.

Second Lieutenant Little heaves a contented sigh, and steps out manfully along the dusty road. Behind him tramp his men. We have no pipers as yet, but melody is supplied by *Tipperary,* sung in ragged chorus, varied by martial interludes upon the mouth-organ. Despise not the mouth-organ. Ours has been a constant boon. It has kept sixty men in step for miles on end.

Fortunately the weather is glorious. Day after day, after a sharp and frosty dawn, the sun swings up into a cloudless sky; and the hundred thousand troops that swarm like ants upon the undulating plains of Hampshire can march, sit, lie, or sleep on hard, sun-baked earth. A wet autumn would have thrown our training back months. The men, as yet, possess nothing but the fatigue uniforms they stand up in, so it is imperative to keep them dry.

Tramp, tramp, tramp. *Tipperary* has died away. The owner of the mouth-organ is temporarily deflated.

Here is an opportunity for individual enterprise. It is soon seized. A husky soloist breaks into one of the deathless ditties of the new Scottish Laureate; his comrades take up the air with ready response; and presently we are all swinging along to the strains of *I Love a Lassie* — *Roaming in the Gloaming* and *It's Just Like Being at Hame* being rendered as encores.

Then presently comes snatches of a humorously amorous nature — *Hallo, Hallo, Who's Your Lady Friend?; You're my Baby;* and the ungrammatical *Who Were You With Last Night?* Another great favourite is an involved composition which always appears to begin in the middle. It deals severely with the precocity of a youthful lover who has been detected wooing his lady in the Park. Each verse ends, with enormous gusto —

"Hold your haand *oot*, you naughty boy!"

Tramp, tramp, tramp. Now we are passing through a village. The inhabitants line the pavement and smile cheerfully upon us — they are always kindly disposed toward "Scotchies" — but the united gaze of the rank and file wanders instinctively from the pavement towards upper windows and kitchen entrances where the domestic staff may be discerned, bunched together and giggling. Now we are out on the road again, silent and dusty. Suddenly, far in the rear, a voice of singular sweetness strikes up *The Banks of Loch Lomond*. Man after man joins in, until the swelling chorus runs from end to end of the long column. Half the battalion hail from the Loch Lomond district, and of the rest there is hardly a man who has not indulged, during some Trades' Holiday or other, in "a pleesure trup" upon its historic but inexpensive waters.

"You'll tak' the high road and I'll tak the low road —"

On we swing, full-throated. An English battalion, halted at a cross-road to let us go by, gazes curiously upon us. *Tipperary* they know, Harry Lauder they have heard of; but this song has no meaning for them. It is ours, ours, ours. So we march on. The feet of Bobby Little, as he tramps at the head of his platoon, hardly touch the ground. His head is in the air. One day, he feels instinctively, he will hear that song again, amid sterner surroundings. When that day comes, the song, please God, for all its sorrowful wording, will reflect no sorrow from the hearts of those who sing it — only courage, and the joy of battle, and the knowledge of victory.

" — And I'll be in Scotland before ye.
But me and my true love will never meet again
On the bonny, bonny *baanks* —"

A shrill whistle sounds far ahead. It means "March at Attention". *Loch Lomond* dies away with uncanny suddenness — discipline is waxing stronger every day — and tunics are buttoned and rifles unslung. Three minutes later we swing demurely on to the barrack square, across which a pleasant aroma of stewed onions is wafting, and deploy with creditable precision into the formation known as "mass". Then comes much dressing of ranks and adjusting of distances. The Colonel is very particular about a clean finish to any piece of work.

Presently the four companies are aligned: the N.C.O.'s retire to the supernumerary ranks. The battalion stands rigid, facing a motionless figure upon horseback. The figure stirs.

"Fall out, the officers!"

They come trooping, stand fast, and salute — very smartly. We must set an example to the men. Besides, we are hungry too.

"Battalion, slope *arms!* Dis—*miss!*"

Every man, with one or two incurable exceptions, turns sharply to his right and cheerfully smacks the butt of his rifle with his disengaged hand. The Colonel gravely returns the salute; and we stream away, all the thousand of us, in the direction of the savoury smell. Two o'clock will come round all too soon, and with it company drill and tiresome musketry exercises; but by that time we shall have *dined,* and Fate cannot touch us for another twenty-four hours.

CHAPTER THREE

GROWING PAINS

WE HAVE OUR little worries of course.

Last week we were all vaccinated, and we did not like it. Most of us have "taken" very severely, which is a sign that we badly needed vaccinating, but makes the discomfort no easier to endure. It is no joke handling a rifle when your left arm is swelled to the full compass of your sleeve, and the personal contact of your neighbour in the ranks is sheer agony. However, officers are considerate, and the work is made as light as possible. The faint-hearted report themselves sick; but the Medical Officer, an unsentimental man of coarse mental fibre, who was on a panel before he heard his country calling, merely recommends them to get well as soon as possible, as they are going to be inoculated for enteric next week. So we grouse — and bear it.

There are other rifts within the military lute. At home we are persons of some consequence, with very definite notions about the dignity of labour. We have employers who tremble at our frown; we have Trades Union officials who are at constant pains to impress upon us our own omnipotence in the industrial world in which we live. We have at our beck and call a Radical M.P. who, in return for our vote and suffrage, informs us that we are the backbone of the nation, and that we must on no account permit ourselves to be trampled upon by the effete and tyrannical upper classes. Finally, we are Scotsmen, with all a Scotsman's curious reserve and contempt for social airs and graces.

But in the Army we appear to be nobody. We are expected to stand stiffly at attention when addressed by an officer; even to call him "sir" — an honour to which our previous employer has been a stranger. At home, if we happened to meet the head of the firm in the street, and none of our colleagues was looking, we touched a cap, furtively. Now, we have no option in the matter. We are expected to degrade ourselves by meaningless and humiliating gestures. The N.C.O.'s are almost as bad. If you answer a sergeant as you would a foreman, you are impertinent; if you argue with him, as all good Scotsmen must, you are insubordinate; if you endeavour to drive a collective bargain with him, you are mutinous; and you are reminded that upon active service mutiny is punishable by death. It is all very unusual and upsetting.

You may not spit; neither may you smoke a cigarette in the ranks, nor keep the residue thereof behind your ear. You may not take beer to bed with you. You may not postpone your shave till Saturday: you must shave every day. You must keep your buttons, accoutrements, and rifle speckless, and have you hair cut in a style which is not becoming to your particular type of beauty. Even your feet are not your own. Every Sunday morning a young officer, whose leave has been specially stopped for the purpose, comes round the barrack-rooms after church and inspects your extremities, revelling in blackened nails and gloating over hammertoes. For all practical purposes, decides Private Mucklewame, you might as well be in Siberia.

Still, one can get used to anything. Our lot is mitigated, too, by the knowledge that we are all in the same boat. The most olympian N.C.O. stands like a ramrod when addressing an officer, while lieutenants make obeisance to a company commander as humbly as any private. Even the Colonel was seen one day to salute an old gentleman who rode on to the parade-ground during morning drill, wearing a red band round his hat. Noting this, we realise that the Army is not, after all, as we first suspected, divided into two classes — oppressors and oppressed. We all have to "go through it".

Presently fresh air, hard training, and clean living begin to weave their spell. Incredulous at first, we find ourselves slowly recognising the fact that it is possible to treat an officer deferentially, or carry out an order smartly, without losing one's self-respect as a man and a Trades Unionist. The insidious habit of cleanliness, once acquired, takes despotic possession of its victims: we find ourselves looking askance at room-mates who have not yet yielded to such predilections. The swimming-bath where once we flapped unwillingly and ingloriously at the shallow end, becomes quite a desirable resort, and we look forward to our weekly visit with something approaching eagerness. We begin, too, to take our profession seriously. Formerly we regarded outpost exercises, advanced guards, and the like, as a rather fatuous form of play-acting, designed to amuse those officers who carry maps and note-books. Now we begin to consider these diversions on their merits, and seriously criticise Second Lieutenant Little for having last night posted one of his sentry groups upon the skyline. Thus is the soul of a soldier born.

We are getting less individualistic, too. We are beginning to think more of our regiment and less of ourselves. At first this loyalty takes the form of criticising other regiments, because their marching is slovenly, or their accoutrements dirty, or — most significant sign of all — their discipline is bad. We are especially critical of our own Eighth Battalion, which is fully three weeks younger than we are, and is not in the First Hundred Thousand at all. In their presence we are war-worn veterans. We express it as our opinion that the officers of some of these battalions must be a poor lot. From this it suddenly comes home to us that our officers are a good lot, and we find ourselves taking a queer pride in our company commander's homely strictures and severe sentences the morning after pay-night. Here is another step in the quickening life of the regiment. *Esprit de corps* is raising its head, class prejudice and our "independence" notwithstanding.

Again, a timely hint dropped by the Colonel on battalion parade this morning has set us thinking. We begin to wonder how we shall compare with the first-line regiments when we find ourselves "oot there". Silently we resolve that when we, the first of the Service Battalions, take our place in trench or firing line alongside the Old Regiment, no one shall be found to draw unfavourable comparisons between parent and offspring. We intend to show ourselves chips of the old block. No one who knows the old regiment can ask more of a young battalion than *that*.

CHAPTER FOUR

THE CONVERSION OF
PRIVATE McSLATTERY

ONE EVENING a rumour ran round the barracks. Most barrack rumours die a natural death, but this one was confirmed by the fact that the next morning the whole battalion, instead of performing the usual platoon exercises, was told off for instruction in the art of presenting arms. "A" company discussed the potent at breakfast.

"What kin' o' a thing is a Review?" inquired Private McSlattery.

Private Mucklewame explained. Private McSlattery was not impressed, and said so quite frankly. In the lower walks of the industrial world Royalty is too often a mere name. Personal enthusiasm for a Sovereign whom they have never seen, and who in their minds is inextricably mixed up with the House of Lords, and capitalism, and the police, is impossible to individuals of the stamp of Private McSlattery. To such, Royalty is simply the head and corner-stone of a legal system which officially prevents a man from being drunk and disorderly, and the British Empire an expensive luxury for which the working man pays while the idle rich draw the profits.

If McSlattery's opinion of the Civil Code was low, his opinion of Military Law was at zero. In his previous existence in his native Clydebank, when weary of rivet-heating and desirous of change and rest, he had been accustomed to take a day off and become pleasantly intoxicated, being comfortably able to afford the loss of pay involved by his absence. On these occasions he was accustomed to sleep off his potations in some public place — usually upon the pavement outside his last house of call — and it was his boast that so long as nobody interfered with him he interfered with nobody. To this attitude the tolerant police force of Clydebank assented, having their hands full enough as a rule, in dealing with more militant forms of alcoholism. But Private McSlattery, No. 3891, soon realised that he and Mr. Matthew McSlattery, rivet-heater and respected citizen of Clydebank, had nothing in common. Only last week, feeling pleasantly fatigued after five days of arduous military training, he had followed the invariable practice of his civil life, and taken a day off. The result had fairly staggered him. In the orderly-room upon Monday morning he was charged with —

(1) Being absent from Parade at 9.00 a.m. on Saturday.
(2) Being absent from Parade at 2.00 p.m. on Saturday.
(3) Being absent from Tattoo at 9.30 p.m. on Saturday.
(4) Being drunk in High Street about 9.40 p.m. on Saturday.
(5) Striking a Non-Commissioned Officer.
(6) Attempting to escape from his escort.
(7) Destroying Government property. (Three panes of glass in the guard-room.)

Private McSlattery, asked for an explanation, had pointed out that if he had been treated as per his working arrangement with the police at Clydebank, there would have been no trouble whatever. As for his day off, he was willing to forgo his day's pay and call the thing square. However, a hidebound C.O. had fined him five shillings and sentenced him to seven days' C.B. Consequently he was in no mood for Royal Reviews. He stated his opinions upon the subject in a loud voice and at some length. No one contradicted him, for he possessed the straightest left in the company; and no dog barked even when McSlattery said that black was white.

"I wunner ye jined the Airmy at all, McSlattery," observed one bold spirit, when the orator paused for breath.

"I wunner myself," said McSlattery simply. "If I had kent all aboot this 'attention' and 'stan'-at-ease', and needin' tae luft your hand tae your bunnet whenever you saw yin o' they gentry-pups of officers goin' by — dagont if I'd hae done it, Germans or no! (But I had a dram in me at the time.) I'm weel kent in Clydebank, and they'll tell you there that I'm no' the man to be wastin' my time presenting airms tae kings or any other bodies."

However, at the appointed hour McSlattery, in the front rank of A Company, stood to attention because he had to, and presented arms very creditably. He now cherished a fresh grievance, for he objected upon principle to have to present arms to a motor-car standing two hundred yards away upon his right front.

"Wull we be gettin' hame to our dinners now!" he inquired gruffly of his neighbour.

"Maybe he'll tak' a closer look at us," suggested an optimist in the rear rank. "He micht walk doon the line."

"Walk! No him!" replied Private McSlattery. "He'll be awa' hame in the motor. Hae ony o' you billies gotten a fag?"

There was a smothered laugh. The officers of the battalion were standing rigidly at attention in front of

A Company. One of these turned his head sharply.

"No talking in the ranks there!" he said. "Sergeant, take that man's name."

Private McSlattery, rumbling mutiny, subsided, and devoted his attention to the movements of the Royal motor-car.

Then the miracle happened.

The great car rolled smoothly from the saluting base, over the undulating turf, and came to a standstill on the extreme right of the line, half a mile away. There descended a slight figure in khaki. It was the King — the King whom Private McSlattery had never seen. Another figure followed, and another.

"Herself iss there too!" whinnied an excited Highlander on McSlattery's right. "And the young leddy! Pless me, they are all for walking town the line on their feet. And the sun so hot in the sky! We shall see them close!"

Private McSlattery gave a contemptuous sniff.

The excited battalion was called to a sense of duty by the voice of authority. Once more the long lines stood stiff and rigid — waiting, waiting, for their brief glimpse. It was a long time coming, for they were posted on the extreme left.

Suddenly a strangled voice was uplifted —

"In God's name, what for can they no' come tae *us?* Never heed the others!"

Yet Private McSlattery was quite unaware that he had spoken.

At last the little procession arrived. There was a handshake for the Colonel, and a word with two or three of the officers; then a quick scrutiny of the rank and file. For a moment — yea, more than a moment — keen Royal eyes rested upon Private McSlattery, standing like a graven image, with his great chest straining the buttons of his tunic.

Then a voice said, apparently in McSlattery's ear —

21

"A magnificent body of men, Colonel. I congratulate you."

A minute later McSlattery was aroused from his trance by the sound of the Colonel's ringing voice —

"Highlanders, three cheers for His Majesty the King!"

McSlattery led the whole Battalion, his glengarry high in the air.

Suddenly his eye fell upon Private Mucklewame, blindly and woodenly yelling himself hoarse.

In three strides McSlattery was standing face to face with the unconscious criminal.

"Yous low, lousy puddock," he roared — "tak' off your bunnet!" He saved Mucklewame the trouble of complying, and strode back to his place in the ranks.

"Yin mair, chaps," he shouted — "for the young leddy!"

And yet there are people who tell us that the formula, O.H.M.S., is a mere relic of antiquity.

CHAPTER FIVE

"CRIME"

"BRING IN PRIVATE DUNSHIE, Sergeant-Major," says the Company Commander.

The Sergeant-Major throws open the door, and barks —

"Private Dunshie's escort!"

The order is repeated *fortissimo* by someone outside. There is a clatter of ammunition boots getting into step, and a solemn procession of four files into the room. The leader thereof is a stumpy but enormously important-looking private. He is the escort. Number two is the prisoner. Numbers three and four are the accuser — counsel for the Crown, as it were — and a witness. The procession reaches the table at which the Captain is sitting. Beside him is a young officer, one Bobby Little, who is present for "instructional" purposes.

"Mark time!" commands the Sergeant-Major. "Halt! Right turn!"

This evolution brings the accused face to face with his judge. He has been deprived of his cap, and of everything else "which may be employed as, or contain, a missile". (They think of everything in the King's Regulations.)

"What is this man's crime, Sergeant-Major?" inquires the Captain.

"On this sheet, sir," replies the Sergeant-Major . . .

23

By a "crime" the ordinary civilian means something worth recording in a special edition of the evening papers – something with a meat-chopper in it. Others, more catholic in their views, will tell you that it is a crime to inflict corporal punishment on any human being; or to permit performing animals to appear upon the stage; or to subsist upon any food but nuts. Others, of still finer clay, will classify such things as Futurism, The Tango, Dickeys, and the Albert Memorial as crimes. The point to note is, that in the eyes of all these persons each of these things is a sin of the worst possible degree. That being so, they designate it a "crime". It is the strongest term they can employ.

But in the Army, "crime" is capable of infinite shades of intensity. It simply means "misdemeanour", and may range from being unshaven on parade, or making a frivolous complaint about the potatoes at dinner, to irrevocably perforating your rival in love with a bayonet. So let party politicians, when they discourse vaguely to their constituents about "the prevalence of crime in the Army under the present effete and undemocratic system", walk warily.

Every private in the Army possesses what is called a conduct-sheet, and upon this his crimes are recorded. To be precise, he has two such sheets. One is called his Company sheet, and the other his Regimental sheet. His Company sheet contains a record of every misdeed for which he has been brought before his Company Commander. His Regimental sheet is a more select document, and contains only the more noteworthy of his achievements — crimes so interesting that they have to be communicated to the Commanding Officer.

However, this morning we are concerned only with Company conduct-sheets. It is 7.30 a.m. and the Company Commander is sitting in judgement, with a little pile of yellow Army forms before him. He picks up the first of these and reads —

"*Private Dunshie. While on active service, refusing to obey an order.* Lance-Corporal Ness!"

The figure upon the prisoner's right suddenly becomes animated. Lance-Corporal Ness, taking a deep breath, and fixing his eyes resolutely on the whitewashed wall above the Captain's head, recites —

"Sirr, at four p.m. on the fufth unst. I was in charge of a party told off for tae scrub the floor of Room Nummer Seeventeen. I ordered the prisoner tae scrub. He refused. I warned him. He again refused."

Click! Lance-Corporal Ness has run down. He has just managed the sentence in a breath.

"Corporal Mackay!"

The figure upon Lance-Corporal Ness's right stiffens, and inflates itself.

"Sirr, on the fufth unst. I was Orderly Sergeant. At aboot four-thirrty p.m., Lance-Corporal Ness reported this man tae me for refusing for to obey an order. I confined him."

The Captain turns to the prisoner.

"What have you to say, Private Dunshie?"

Private Dunshie, it appears, has a good deal to say.

"I jined the Airmy for tae fight they Germans, and no' for tae be learned tae scrub floors —"

"Sirr!" suggests the Sergeant-Major in his ear.

"Sirr!" amends Private Dunshie reluctantly. "I was no' in the habit of scrubbin' the floor mysel' where I stay in Glesca'; and ma wife would be affronted —"

But the Captain looks up. He has heard enough.

"Look here, Dunshie," he says. "Glad to hear you want to fight the Germans. So do I. So do we all. All the same, we've got a lot of dull jobs to do first." (Captain Blaikie has the reputation of being the most monosyllabic man in the British Army.) "Coals, and floors, and fatigues like that: they are your job. I have mine too. Kept me up till two this morning. But the point is this. You have refused to obey an order. Very serious, that.

Most serious crime a soldier can commit. If you start arguing now about small things, where will you be when the big orders come along — eh? Must learn to obey. Soldier now, whatever you were a month ago. So obey all orders like a shot. Watch me next time I get one. No disgrace, you know! Ought to be a soldier's pride, and all that. See?"

"Yes — sirr," replies Private Dunshie, with less truculence.

The Captain glances down at the paper before him.

"First time you have come before me. Admonished!"

"Right turn! Quick march!" thunders the Sergeant-Major.

The procession clumps out of the room. The Captain turns to his disciple.

"That's my homely and paternal tap," he observes. "For first offenders only. That chap's all right. Soon find out it's no good fussing about your rights as a true-born British elector in the Army. Sergeant-Major!"

"Sirr?"

"Private McNulty!"

After the usual formalities, enter Private McNulty and escort. Private McNulty is a small scared-looking man with a dirty face.

"Private McNulty, sirr!" announces the Sergeant-Major to the Company Commander, with the air of a popular lecturer on entomology placing a fresh insect under the microscope.

Captain Blaikie addresses the shivering culprit —

"Private McNulty; charged with destroying Government property. Corporal Mather!"

Corporal Mather clears his throat, and assuming the wooden expression and fish-like gaze common to all public speakers who have learned their oration by heart, begins —

"Sirr, on the night of the sixth inst. I was Orderly Sergeant. Going round the prisoner's room about the hour of nine-thirty I noticed that his three biscuits had been cut and slashed, apparently with a knife or other instrument."

"What did you do?"

"Sirr, I inquired of the men in the room who was it had gone for to do this. Sirr, they said it was the prisoner."

Two witnesses are called. Both certify, casting grieved and virtuous glances at the prisoner, that this outrage upon the property of His Majesty was the work of Private McNulty.

To the unsophisticated Bobby Little this charge appears rather a frivolous one. If you may not cut or slash a biscuit, what *are* you to do with it? Swallow it whole?

"Private McNulty?" queries the Captain.

Private McNulty, in a voice which is shrill with righteous indignation, gives the somewhat unexpected answer —

"Sirr, I plead guilty!"

"Guilty — eh? You did it, then?"

"Yes, sir."

"Why?"

This is what Private McNulty is waiting for.

"The men in that room, sirr," he announces indignantly, "appear tae look on me as a sort of body that can be treated onyways. They go for tae aggravate me. I was sittin' on my bed, with my knife in my hand, cutting a piece bacca and interfering with naebody, when they all commenced tae fling biscuits at me. I was keepin' them off as weel as I could; but havin' a knife in my hand, I'll no deny what I gave twa three of them a bit cut."

"Is this true?" asks the Captain of the first witness curtly.

"Yes, sir."

"You saw the men throwing biscuits at the prisoner?"

"Yes, sir."

"He was daen' it himsel'!" proclaims Private McNulty.

"This true?"

"Yes, sir."

The Captain addresses the other witness.

"You doing it too?"

"Yes, sir."

The Captain turns again to the prisoner.

"Why didn't you lodge a complaint?" (The school-boy code does not obtain in the Army.)

"I did, sir. I tellt" — indicating Corporal Mather with an elbow — "this genelman here."

Corporal Mather cannot help it. He swells percepti-bly. But swift puncture awaits him.

"Corporal Mather, why didn't you mention this?"

"I didna think it affected the crime, sir."

"Not your business to think. Only to make a straight-forward charge. Be very careful in future. You other two" — the witnesses come guiltily to attention — "I shall talk to your platoon sergeant about you. Not going to have Government property knocked about!"

Bobby Little's eyebrows, willy-nilly, have been steadily rising during the last five minutes. He knows the meaning of red tape now!

Then comes sentence.

"Private McNulty, you have pleaded guilty to a charge of destroying Government property, so you go before the Commanding Officer. Don't suppose you'll be punished, beyond paying for the damage."

"Right turn! Quick march!" chants the Sergeant-Major.

The downtrodden McNulty disappears, with his traducers. But Bobby Little's eyebrows have not been altogether thrown away upon his Company Com-mander.

"Got the biscuits here, Sergeant-Major?"

"Yes, sirr."

"Show them."

The Sergeant-Major dives into a pile of brown blankets, and presently extracts three small brown mattresses, each two feet square. These appear to have been stabbed in several places with a knife.

Captain Blaikie's eyes twinkle, and he chuckles to his now scarlet-faced junior —

"More biscuits in heaven and earth than ever came out of Huntley and Palmer's, my son! Private Robb!"

Presently Private Robb stands at the table. He is a fresh-faced, well-set-up youth, with a slightly receding chin and a most dejected manner.

"Private Robb," reads the Captain. *"While on active service, drunk and singing in Wellington Street about nine p.m. on Saturday the sixth.* Sergeant Garrett!"

The proceedings follow their usual course, except that in this case some of the evidence is "documentary" — put in in the form of a report from the Sergeant of the Military Police who escorted the melodious Robb home to bed.

The Captain addresses the prisoner.

"Private Robb, this is the second time. Sorry — very sorry. In all other ways you are doing well. Very keen and promising soldier. Why is it — eh?"

The contrite Robb hangs his head. His judge continues —

"I'll tell you. You haven't found out yet how much you can hold. That it?"

The prisoner nods assent.

"Well — find out! See? It's one of the first things a young man ought to learn. Very valuable piece of information. I know myself, so I'm safe. Want you to do the same. Every man has a different limit. What did you have on Saturday?"

Private Robb reflects.

"Five pints, sirr," he announces.

"Well, next time try three, and then you won't go serenading policemen. As it is, you will have to go before the Commanding Officer and get punished. Want to go to the front, don't you?"

"Yes, sirr." Private Robb's dismal features flush.

"Well, mind this. We all want to go, but we can't go till every man in the battalion is efficient. You want to be the man who kept the rest from going to the front — eh?"

"No, sirr, I do not."

"All right, then. Next Saturday night say to yourself: 'Another pint, and I keep the Battalion back!' If you do that, you'll come back to barracks sober, like a decent chap. That'll do. Don't salute with your cap off. Next man, Sergeant-Major!"

"Good boy, that," remarks the Captain to Bobby Little, as the contrite Robb is removed. "Keen as mustard. But his high-water mark for beer is somewhere in his boots. All right, now I've scared him."

"Last prisoner, sirr," announces the Sergeant-Major.

"Glad to hear it. H'm! Private M'Queen again!"

Private M'Queen is an unpleasant-looking creature, with a drooping red moustache and a cheese-coloured complexion. His misdeeds are recited. Having been punished for misconduct early in the week, he has piled Pelion on Ossa by appearing fighting drunk at defaulters' parade. From all accounts he has livened up that usually decorous assemblage considerably.

After the corroborative evidence, the Captain asks his usual question of the prisoner —

"Anything to say?"

"No," growls Private M'Queen.

The Captain takes up the prisoner's conduct-sheet, reads it through, and folds it up deliberately.

"I am going to ask the Commanding Officer to discharge you," he says; and there is nothing homely or paternal in his speech now. "Can't make out why men like you join the Army — especially *this* Army. Been a nuisance ever since you came here. Drunk — beastly drunk — four times in three weeks. Always dirty and insubordinate. Always trying to stir up trouble among the young soldiers. Been in the army before, haven't you?"

"No."

"That's not true. Can always tell an old soldier on parade. Fact is, you have either deserted or been discharged as incorrigible. Going to be discharged as incorrigible again. Keeping the regiment back, that's why: that's a real crime. Go home, and explain that you were turned out of the King's Army because you weren't worthy of the honour of staying in. When decent men see that people like you have no place in this regiment, perhaps they will see that this regiment is just the place for them. Take him away."

Private M'Queen shambles out of the room for the last time in his life. Captain Blaikie, a little exhausted by his own unusual loquacity, turns to Bobby Little with a contented sigh.

"That's the last of the shysters," he says. "Been weeding them out for six weeks. Now I have got rid of that nobleman I can look the rest of the Company in the face. Come to breakfast!"

CHAPTER SIX

THE LAWS OF THE
MEDES AND PERSIANS

ONE'S FIRST DAYS as a newly-joined subaltern are very like one's first days at school. The feeling is just the same. There is the same natural shyness, the same reverence for people who afterwards turn out to be of no consequence whatsoever, and the same fear of transgressing the Laws of the Medes and Persians — regimental traditions and conventions - which alter not.

Dress, for instance. "Does one wear a sword on parade?" asks the tyro of himself his first morning. "I'll put it on, and chance it." He invests himself in a monstrous claymore and steps on to the barrack square. Not an officer in sight is carrying anything more lethal than a light cane. There is just time to scuttle back to quarters and disarm.

Again, where should one sit at meal-times? We had supposed that the C.O. would be enthroned at the head of the table, with a major sitting on his right and left, like Cherubim and Seraphim; while the rest disposed themselves in a descending scale of greatness until it came down to persons like ourselves at the very foot. But the C.O. has a disconcerting habit of sitting absolutely anywhere. He appears to be just as happy between two Second Lieutenants as between Cherubim and Seraphim. Again, we note that at breakfast each officer upon entering sits down and shouts loudly, to a being concealed behind a screen, for food, which is speedily forthcoming. Are we entitled to clamour in this peremptory fashion too? Or should we creep round behind the screen and take what we can get? Or should we sit still, and wait till we are served? We try the last expedient first, and get nothing. Then we try the second, and are speedily convinced, by the demeanour of the gentlemen behind the screen, that we have committed the worst error of which we have yet been guilty.

There are other problems — saluting, for instance. On the parade-ground this is a simple matter enough; for there the golden rule appears to be — When in doubt, salute! The Colonel calls up his four Company Commanders. They salute. He instructs them to carry on this morning with coal fatigues and floor-scrubbing. The Company Commanders salute, and retire to their Companies, and call up their subalterns, who salute. They instruct these to carry on this morning with coal fatigues and floor-scrubbing. The sixteen subalterns salute, and retire to their platoons. Here they call up their Platoon Sergeants, who salute. They instruct these to carry on this morning with coal fatigues and floor-scrubbing. The Platoon Sergeants salute, and issue commands to the rank and file. The rank and file, having no instructions to salute sergeants, are compelled, as a last resort, to carry on with the coal fatigues and floor-scrubbing themselves. You see, on parade saluting is simplicity itself.

But we are not always on parade; and then more subtle problems arise. Some of those were discussed one day by four junior officers, who sat upon a damp and slippery bank by a muddy roadside during a "fall-out" in a route-march. The four ("reading from left to right", as they say in high journalistic society) were Second Lieutenant Little, Second Lieutenant Waddell,

Second Lieutenant Cockerell, and Lieutenant Struthers, surnamed "Highbrow". Bobby we know. Waddell was a slow-moving but pertinacious student of the science of war from the kingdom of Fife. Cockerell came straight from a crack public-school corps, where he had been a cadet officer; so nothing in the heaven above or the earth beneath was hid from him. Struthers owed his superior rank to the fact that in the far back ages, before the days of the O.T.C., he had held a commission in a University Corps. He was a scholar of his College, and was an expert in the art of accumulating masses of knowledge in quick time for examination purposes. He knew all the little red manuals by heart, was an infallible authority on buttons and badges, and would dip into the King's Regulations or the Field Service Pocket-book as another man might dip into *The Sporting Times*. Strange to say, he was not very good at drilling a platoon. We all know him.

"What do you do when you are leading a party along a road and meet a Staff Officer?" asked Bobby Little.

"Make a point," replied Cockerell patronisingly, "of saluting all persons wearing red bands round their hats. They may not be entitled to it, but it tickles their ribs and gets you the reputation of being an intelligent young officer."

"But I say," announced Waddell plaintively, "*I* saluted a man with a red hat the other day, and he turned out to be a Military Policeman!"

"As a matter of fact," announced the pundit Struthers, after the laughter had subsided, "you need not salute anybody. No compliments are paid on active service, and we are on active service now."

"Yes, but suppose some one salutes *you?*"objected the conscientious Bobby Little. "You must salute back again, and sometimes you don't know how to do it. The other day I was bringing the company back from the ranges and we met a company from another battalion

— the Mid Mudshires, I think. Before I knew where I was the fellow in charge called them to attention and then gave 'Eyes right!'"

"What did you do?" asked Struthers anxiously.

"I hadn't time to do anything except grin, and say 'Good morning!'" confessed Bobby Little.

"You were perfectly right," announced Struthers, and Còckerell murmured assent.

"Are you sure?" persisted Bobby Little. "As I passed the tail of their company one of their subs turned to another and said quite loud, 'My God, what swine!'"

"Showed his rotten ignorance," commented Cockerell.

At this moment Mr Waddell, whose thoughts were never disturbed by conversation around him, broke in with a question.

"What does a Tommy do," he inquired, "if he meets an officer wheeling a wheelbarrow?"

"Who is wheeling the barrow," inquired the meticulous Struthers — "the officer or the Tommy?"

"The Tommy, of course!" replied Waddell in quite a shocked voice. "What is he to do? If he tries to salute he will upset the barrow, you know."

"He turns his head sharply towards the officer for six paces," explained the ever-ready Struthers. "When a soldier is not in a position to salute in the ordinary way —"

"I say," inquired Bobby Little rather shyly, "do you ever look the other way when you meet a Tommy?"

"How do you mean?" asked everybody.

"Well, the other day I met one walking out with his girl along the road, and I felt so blooming *de trop* that —"

Here the "fall-in" sounded, and this delicate problem was left unsolved. But Mr Waddell, who liked to get to the bottom of things, continued to ponder these matters as he marched. He mistrusted the omniscience of Struthers and the superficial infallibility of the self-satisfied Cockerell. Accordingly, after consultation with that eager searcher after knowledge, Second Lieutenant Little, he took the laudable but fatal step of carrying his difficulties to one Captain Wagstaffe, the humorist of the Battalion.

Wagstaffe listened with an appearance of absorbed interest. Finally he said —

"These are very important questions, Mr Waddell, and you acted quite rightly in laying them before me. I will consult the Deputy Assistant Instructor in Military Etiquette, and will obtain a written answer to your inquiries."

"Oh, thanks awfully sir!" exclaimed Waddell.

The result of Captain Wagstaffe's application to the mysterious official just designated was forthcoming next day in the form of a neatly typed document. It was posted in the Ante-room (the C.O. being out at dinner), and ran as follows:

SALUTES

YOUNG OFFICERS, HINTS FOR THE GUIDANCE OF

The following is the correct procedure for a young officer in charge of an armed party upon meeting —

(a) A Staff Officer riding a bicycle.

Correct Procedure. — If marching at attention, order your men to march at ease and to light cigarettes and eat bananas. Then, having fixed bayonets, give the order: *Across the road — straggle!*

(b) A funeral.

Correct Procedure. — Strike up *Tipperary,* and look the other way.

(c) A General Officer, who strolls across your Barrack Square precisely at the moment when you and your Platoon have got into mutual difficulties.

Correct Procedure. — Lie down flat upon your face (directing your platoon to do the same), cover your head with gravel, and pretend you are not there.

(a) A soldier, wheeling a wheelbarrow and balancing a swill-tub on his head, meets an officer walking out in review dress.

Correct Procedure. — The soldier will immediately cant the swill-tub to an angle of forty-five degrees, at a distance of one and a half inches above his right eyebrow. (In the case of Rifle Regiments the soldier will balance the swill-tub on his nose.) He will then invite the officer, by a smart movement of the left ear, to seat himself on the wheelbarrow.

Correct Acknowledgment. — The officer will comply, placing his feet upon the right and left hubs of the wheel respectively, with the ball of the toe in each case at a distance of one inch (when serving abroad, $2\frac{1}{2}$ centimetres) from the centre of gravity of the wheelbarrow. (In the case of Rifle Regiments the officer will tie his feet in a knot at the back of his neck.) The soldier will then advance six paces, after which the officer will dismount and go home and have a bath.

(b) A soldier, with his arm round a lady's waist in the gloaming, encounters an officer.

Correct Procedure. — The soldier will salute with his disengaged arm. The lady will administer a sharp tap with the end of her umbrella to the officer's tunic, at point one inch above the lowest button.

Correct Acknowledgment. — The officer will take the end of the umbrella firmly in his right hand, and will require the soldier to introduce him to the lady. He will then direct the soldier to double back to barracks.

(c) A party of soldiers, seated upon the top of a transport wagon, see an officer passing at the side of the road.

Correct Procedure. — The senior N.C.O. (or if no N.C.O. be present, the oldest soldier) will call the men to attention, and the party, taking their time from the right, will spit upon the officer's head in a soldier-like manner.

Correct Acknowledgment. — The officer will break into a smart trot.

(d) A soldier, driving an officer's motor-car without the knowledge of the officer, encounters the officer in a narrow country lane.

Correct Procedure. — The soldier will open the throttle to its full extent and run the officer over.

Correct Acknowledgment. — No acknowledgment is required.

NOTE – *None of the above compliments will be paid upon active service.*

Unfortunately the Colonel came home from dining out sooner than was expected, and found this outrageous document still upon the noticeboard. But he was a good Colonel. He merely remarked approvingly —

"H'm. Quite so! *Non semper arcum tendit Apollo.* It's just as well to keep smiling these days."

Nevertheless, Mr Waddell made a point in future, when in need of information, of seeking the same from a less inspired source than Captain Wagstaffe.

There was another Law of the Medes and Persians with which our four friends soon became familiar — that which governs the relations of the various ranks to one another. Great Britain is essentially the home of the chaperon. We pride ourselves, as a nation, upon the extreme care with which we protect our young gentlewomen from contaminating influences. But the fastidious attention which we bestow upon our national maidenhood is as nothing in comparison with the protective commotion with which we surround that shrinking sensitive plant, Mr Thomas Atkins.

Take etiquette and deportment. If a soldier wishes to speak to an officer, an introduction must be effected by a sergeant. Let us suppose that Private McSplae, in the course of a route-march, develops a blister upon his great toe. He begins by intimating the fact to the nearest lance-corporal. The lance-corporal takes the news to the platoon sergeant, who informs the platoon commander, who may or may not decide to take the opinion of his company commander in the matter. Anyhow, when the hobbling warrior finally obtains permission to fall out and alleviate his distress, a corporal goes with him, for fear he should lose himself, or his boot — it is wonderful what Thomas *can* lose when he sets his mind to it — or, worst crime of all, his rifle.

Again, if two privates are detailed to empty the regimental ashbin, a junior N.C.O. ranges them in line, calls them to attention, and marches them off to the scene of their labours, decently and in order. If a soldier obtains leave to go home on furlough for the weekend, he is collected into a party, and, after being inspected to see that his buttons are clean, his hair properly cut, and his nose correctly blown, is marched off to the station, where a ticket is provided for him, and he and his fellow-wayfarers are safely tucked into a third-smoker labelled "Military Party". (No wonder he sometimes gets lost on arriving at Waterloo!) In short, if there is a job to be done, the senior soldier present chaperons somebody else while he does it.

The system has been attacked on the ground that it breeds loss of self-reliance and initiative. As a matter of fact, the result is almost exactly the opposite. Under its operation a soldier rapidly acquires the art of placing himself under the command of his nearest superior in rank; but at the same time he learns with equal rapidity to take command himself if no superior be present — no bad thing in times of battle and sudden death, when shrapnel is whistling, and promotion is taking place with grim and unceasing automaticity.

This principle is extended, too, to the enforcement of law and order. If Private McSumph is insubordinate or riotous, there is never any question of informal correction or summary justice. News of the incident wends its way upward, by a series of properly regulated channels, to the officer in command. Presently, by the same route, an order comes back, and in a twinkling the offender finds himself taken under arrest and marched off to the guard-room by two of his own immediate associates. (One of them may be his own rear-rank man.) But no officer or non-commissioned officer ever lays a finger on him. The penalty for striking a superior officer is so severe that the law decrees, very wisely, that a soldier must on no account ever be arrested by any save men of his own rank. If Private McSumph, while being removed in custody, strikes Private Tosh upon the nose and kicks Private Cosh upon the shin, to the effusion of blood, no great harm is done — except to the lacerated Cosh and Tosh; but if he had smitten an intruding officer in the eye, his punishment would have been dire and grim. So, though we may call military law cumbrous and grandmotherly, there is sound sense and real mercy at the root of it.

But there is one Law of the Medes and Persians which is sensibly relaxed these days. We, the newly joined, have always been given to understand that whatever else you do, you must never, never betray any interest in your profession — in short, talk shop — at Mess. But in our Mess no one ever talks anything else. At luncheon, we relate droll anecdotes concerning our infant platoons; at tea, we explain, to any one who will listen, exactly how we placed our sentry line in last night's operations; at dinner, we brag about our Company musketry returns, and quote untruthful extracts from our butt registers. At breakfast, ever one has a newspaper, which he props before him and reads, generally aloud. We exchange observations upon the war news. We criticise von Kluck, and speak kindly of Joffre. We note, daily, that there is nothing to report on the Allies' right, and wonder regularly how the Russians are really getting on in the Eastern theatre.

Then, after observing that the only sportsman in the combined forces of the German Empire is — or was — the captain of the *Emden,* we come to the casualty lists — and there is silence.

Englishmen are fond of saying, with the satisfied air of men letting off a really excellent joke, that every one in Scotland knows everyone else. As we study the morning's Roll of Honour, we realise that never was a more truthful jest uttered. There is not a name in the list of those who have died for Scotland which is not familiar to us. If we did not know the man — too often the boy — himself, we knew his people, or at least where his home was. In England, if you live in Kent, and you read that the Northumberland Fusiliers have been cut up or the Duke of Cornwall's Light Infantry badly knocked about, you merely sigh that so many more good men should have fallen. Their names are glorious names, but they are only names. But never a Scottish regiment comes underfire but the whole of Scotland feels it. Scotland is small enough to know all her sons by heart. You may live in Berwickshire, and the man who has died may have come from Skye; but his name is quite familiar to you. Big England's sorrow is national; little Scotland's is personal.

Then we pass on to our letters. Many of us — particularly the senior officers — have news direct from the trenches — scribbled scraps torn out of field-message books. We get constant tidings of the Old Regiment. They marched thirty-five miles on such a day; they captured a position after being under continuous shell fire for eight hours on another; they were personally thanked by the Field-Marshall on another. Oh, we shall have to work hard to get up to that standard!

"They want more officers," announces the Colonel. "Naturally, after the time they've been having! But they must go to the Third Battalion for them: that's the proper place. I will not have them coming here: I've told them so at Headquarters. The Service Battalions simply *must* be led by the officers who have trained them if they are to have a Chinaman's chance when we go out. I shall threaten to resign if they try any more of their tricks. That'll frighten 'em! Even dug-outs like me are rare and valuable objects at present."

The Company Commanders murmur assent — on the whole sympathetically. Anxious though they are to get upon business terms with the Kaiser, they are loath to abandon the unkempt but sturdy companies over which they have toiled so hard, and which now, though destitute of blossom, are rich in promise of fruit. But the senior subalterns look up hopefully. Their lot is hard. Some of them have been in the Service for ten years, yet they have been left behind. They command no companies. "Here," their faces say, "we are merely marking time while others learn. Send *us!*"

However, though they have taken no officers yet, signs are not wanting that they will take some soon. Today each of us was presented with a small metal disc.

Bobby Little examined his curiously. Upon the face thereof was stamped, in ragged, irregular capitals —

LITTLE, R., 2ND LT.,

B. & W. HIGHRS.

C. OF E.

"What is this for?" he asked.

Captain Wagstaffe answered.

"You wear it round your neck," he said.

Our four friends, once bitten, regarded the humorist suspiciously.

"Are you rotting us?" asked Waddell cautiously.

"No, my son," replied Wagstaffe, "I am not."

"What is it for, then?"

"It's called an Identity Disc. Every soldier on active service wears one."

"Why should the idiots put one's religion on the thing?" inquired Master Cockerell, scornfully regarding the letters "C. of E." upon his disc.

Wagstaffe regarded him curiously.

"Think it over," he suggested.

CHAPTER SEVEN

SHOOTING STRAIGHT

"WHAT FOR IS THE WEE felly gaun' tae show us puctures?"

Second Lieutenant Bobby Little, assisted by a sergeant and two unhandy privates, is engaged in propping a large and highly-coloured work of art, mounted on a rough wooden frame and supported on two unsteady legs, against the wall of the barrack square. A half platoon of A Company, seated upon an adjacent bank, chewing grass and enjoying the mellow autumn sunshine, regard the swaying masterpiece with frank curiosity. For the last fortnight they have been engaged in imbibing the science of musketry. They have learned to hold their rifles correctly, sitting, kneeling, standing, or lying; to bring their backsights and foresights into an undeviating straight line with the base of the bull's-eye; and to press the trigger in the manner laid down in the Musketry Regulations — without wriggling the body or "pulling-off."

They have also learned to adjust their sights, to perform the loading motions rapidly and correctly, and to obey such simple commands as —

"At them twa weemen" — officers' wives, probably — *"proceeding from left tae right across the square, at five hundred yards"* — they are really about fifteen yards away, covered with confusion — *"five roonds, fire!"*

But as yet they have discharged no shots from their

rifles. It has all been make-believe, with dummy cartridges, and fictitious ranges, and snapping triggers. To be quite frank, they are getting just a little tired of musketry training — forgetting for the moment that a soldier who cannot use his rifle is merely an expense to his country and a free gift to the enemy. But the sight of Bobby Little's art gallery cheers them up. They contemplate the picture with childlike interest. It resembles nothing so much as one of those pleasing but imaginative posters by the display of which our Railway Companies seek to attract the tourist to the less remunerative portions of their systems.

"What for is the wee felly gaun' tae show us puctures?"

Thus Private Mucklewame. A pundit in the rear rank answers him.

"Yon's Gairmany."

"Gairmany my auntie!" retorts Mucklewame. "There's no chumney-stalks in Gairmany."

"Maybe no; but there's wundmulls. See the wundmull there — on yon wee knowe!"

"There a pit heid!" exclaims another voice. This homely spectacle is received with an affectionate sigh. Until two months ago more than half the platoon had never been out of sight of at least half a dozen.

"See the kirk, in ablow the brae!" says someone else, in a pleased voice. "It has a nock in the steeple."

"I hear the Gairmans send signals with their kirknocks," remarks Private McMicking, who, as one of the Battalion signallers — or "buzzers", as the vernacular has it, in imitation of the buzzing of the Morse instrument — regards himself as a sort of junior Staff Officer. "They jist semaphore with the haunds of the nock —"

"I wonder," remarks the dreamy voice of Private McLeary, the humorist of the platoon, "did ever a Gairman buzzer pit the ba' through his ain goal in a fitba' match?"

This irrelevant reference to a regrettable incident of the previous Saturday afternoon is greeted with so much laughter that Bobby Little, who has at length fixed his picture in position, whips round.

"Less talking there!" he announces severely, "or I shall have to stand you all at attention!"

There is immediate silence — there is nothing the matter with Bobby's discipline — and the outraged McMicking has to content himself with a homicidal glare in the direction of McLeary, who is now hanging virtuously upon his officer's lips.

"This," proceeds Bobby Little, "is what is known as a landscape target."

He indicates the picture, which, apparently overcome by so much public notice, promptly falls flat upon its face. A fatigue party under the sergeant hurries to its assistance.

"It is intended," resumes Bobby presently, "to teach you — us — to become familiar with various kinds of country, and to get into the habit of picking out conspicuous features of the landscape, and getting them by heart, and — er — so on. I want you all to study this picture for three minutes. Then I shall face you about and ask you to describe it to me."

After three minutes of puckered brows and hard breathing the squad is turned to its rear, and the examination proceeds.

"Lance-Corporal Ness, what did you notice in the foreground of the picture?"

Lance-Corporal Ness gazes fiercely before him. He has noticed a good deal, but can remember nothing. Moreover, he has no very clear idea what a foreground may be.

"Private Mucklewame?"

Again silence, while the rotund Mucklewame perspires in the throes of mental exertion.

"Private Wemyss?"

No answer.

"Private McMicking?"

The "buzzer" smiles feebly, but says nothing.

"Well," — desperately — "Sergeant Angus! Tell them what you noticed in the foreground."

Sergeant Angus (*floruit* A.D. 1895) springs smartly to attention, and replies, with the instant obedience of the old soldier —

"The sky, sirr."

"Not in the foreground, as a rule," replies Bobby Little gently. "About turn again, all of you, and we'll have another try."

In his next attempt Bobby abandons individual catechism.

"Now," he begins, "what conspicuous objects do we notice on this target? In the foreground I can see a low knoll. To the left I see a windmill. In the distance is a tall chimney. Half-right is a church. How would that church be marked on a map?"

No reply.

"Well," explains Bobby, anxious to parade a piece of knowledge which he only acquired himself a day or two ago, "churches are denoted in maps by a cross, mounted on a square or circle, according as the church has a square tower or a steeple. What has this church got?"

"A nock!" bellow the platoon, with stunning enthusiasm. (All but Private McMicking, that is.)

"A clock, sir," translates the sergeant, *sotto voce.*

"A clock? All right: but what I wanted was a steeple. Then, farther away, we can see a mine, a winding brook, and a house, with a wall in front of it. Who can see them?"

To judge by the collective expression of the audience, no one does. Bobby ploughs on.

"Upon the skyline we notice — Squad, *'shun!'*"

Captain Wagstaffe has strolled up. He is second in

command of A Company. Bobby explains to him modestly what he has been trying to do.

"Yes, I heard you," says Wagstaffe. "You take a breather, while I carry on for a bit. Squad, stand easy, and tell me what you can see on that target. Lance-Corporal Ness, show me a pit-head."

Lance-Corporal Ness steps briskly forward and lays a grubby forefinger on Bobby's "mine".

"Private Mucklewame, show me a burn."

The brook is at once identified.

"Private McLeary, shut your eyes and tell me what there is just to the right of the windmill."

"A wee knowe, sirr," replies McLeary at once. Bobby recognises his "low knoll" — also the fact that it is no use endeavouring to instruct the unlettered until you have learned their language.

"Very good!" says Captain Wagstaffe. "Now we will go on to what is known as Description and Recognition of Targets. Supposing I had sent one of you forward into that landscape as a scout. — By the way, what is a scout?"

Dead silence, as usual.

"Come along! Tell me, somebody! Private Mucklewame?"

"They gang oot in a procession on Setterday efternoons, sirr, in short breeks," replies Mucklewame promptly.

"A procession is the very last thing a scout goes out in!" raps Wagstaffe. (It is plain to Mucklewame that the Captain has never been in Wishaw, but he does not argue the point.)

"Private McMicking, what is a scout?"

"A spy, sirr," replies the omniscient one.

"Well, that's better; but there's a big difference between the two. What is it?"

This is a poser. Several men know the difference, but feel quite incapable of explaining it. The question runs down the front rank. Finally it is held up and disposed of by one Mearns (from Aberdeen).

"A spy, sirr, gets mair money than a scout."

"Does he?" asks Captain Wagstaffe, smiling. "Well, I am not in a position to say. But if he does, he earns it! Why?"

"Because if he gets catched he gets shot," volunteers a rear-rank man.

"Right. Why is he shot?"

This conundrum is too deep for the squad. The Captain has to answer it himself.

"Because he is not in uniform, and cannot therefore be treated as an ordinary prisoner of war. So never go scouting in your nightshirt, Mucklewame!"

The respectable Mucklewame blushes deeply at this outrageous suggestion, but Wagstaffe proceeds —

"Now, supposing I sent you out scouting, and you discovered that over there — somewhere in the middle of this field" — he lays a finger on the field in question — "there was a fold in the ground where a machine-gun section was concealed: what would you do when you got back?"

"I would tell you, sirr," replied Private McMicking politely.

"Tell me what?"

"That they was there, sirr."

"Where?"

"In yon place."

"How would you indicate the position of the place?"

"I would pint it oot with ma finger, sirr."

"Invisible objects half a mile away are not easily pointed out with the finger," Captain Wagstaffe mentions. "Lance-Corporal Ness, how would you describe it?"

"I would tak' you there, sirr."

"Thanks! But I doubt if either of us would come back! Private Wemyss?"

"I would say, sirr, that the place was west of the mansion-hoose."

"There's a good deal of land west of that mansion-house, you know," expostulates the Captain gently; "but we are getting on. Thompson?"

"I would say, sirr," replies Thompson, puckering his brow, "that it was in ablow they trees."

"It would be hard to indicate the exact trees you meant. Trees are too common. You try, Corporal King."

But Corporal King, who earned his stripes by reason of physical rather than intellectual attributes, can only contribute a lame reference to "a bit hedge by yon dyke, where there's a kin' o' hole in the tairget". Wagstaffe breaks in —

"Now, everybody, take some conspicuous and unmistakable object about the middle of that landscape — something which no one can mistake. The mansion-house will do — the near end. Now then — *mansion-house, near end!* Got that?"

There is a general chorus of assent.

"Very well. I want you to imagine that the base of the mansion-house is the centre of a great clock-face. Where would twelve o'clock be?"

The platoon are plainly tickled by this new round-game. They reply —

"Straught up!"

"Right. Where is nine o'clock?"

"Over tae the left."

"Very good. And so on with all the other hours. Now, supposing I were to say, *End of mansion-house — six o'clock — white gate* — you would carry your eye straight *downward*, through the garden, until it encountered the gate. I would thus have enabled you to recognise a very small object in a wide landscape in the quickest possible time. See the idea?"

"Yes, sirr."

"All right. Now for our fold in the ground. *End of mansion-house — eight o'clock —* got that?"

There is an interested murmur of assent.

"That gives you the direction from the house. Now for the distance! *End of mansion-house — eight o'clock — two finger-breadths —* what does that give you, Lance-Corporal Ness?"

"The corrner of a field, sirr."

"Right. This is *our* field. We have picked it correctly out of about twenty fields, you see. *Corner of field. In the middle of the field, a fold in the ground. At nine hundred — at the fold in the ground — five rounds — fire!* You see the idea now?"

"Yes, sirr."

"Very good. Let the platoon practise describing targets to one another, Mr Little. Don't be too elaborate. Never employ either the clock or finger method if you can describe your target without. For instance: *Left of windmill — triangular cornfield. At the nearest corner — six hundred — rapid fire!* is all you want. Carry on, Mr Little."

And leaving Bobby and his infant class to practise this new and amusing pastime, Captain Wagstaffe strolls away across the square to where the painstaking Waddell is contending with another squad.

They, too, have a landscape target — a different one. Before it half a dozen rifles stand, set in rests. Waddell has given the order: *Four hundred — at the road, where it passes under the viaduct — fire!* and six privates have laid the six rifles upon the point indicated. Waddell and Captain Wagstaffe walk down the line, peering along the sights of the rifles. Five are correctly aligned: the sixth points to the spacious firmament above the viaduct.

"Hallo!" observes Wagstaffe.

"This is the man's third try, sir," explains the harassed Waddell. "He doesn't seem to be able to distinguish anything at all."

"Eyesight wrong?"

"So he says, sir."

"Been a long time finding out, hasn't he?"

"The sergeant told me, sir," confides Waddell, "that in his opinion the man is 'working for his ticket.'"

"Umph!"

"I did not quite understand the expression, sir," continues the honest youth, "so I thought I would consult you."

"It means that he is trying to get his discharge. Bring him along: I'll soon find out whether he is skrimshanking or not."

Private McSweir is introduced, and led off to the lair of that hardened cynic, the Medical Officer. Here he is put through some simple visual tests. He soon finds himself out of his depth. It is extremely difficult to feign either myopia, hypermetria, or astigmatism if you are not acquainted with the necessary symptoms, and have not decided beforehand which (if any) of these diseases you are suffering from. In five minutes the afflicted McSweir is informed, to his unutterable indignation, that he has passed a severe ocular examination with flying colours, and is forthwith marched back to his squad, with instructions to recognise all targets in future, under pain of special instruction in the laws of optics during his leisure hours. Verily, in K (1) — that is the tabloid title of the First Hundred Thousand — the way of the malingerer is hard.

Still, the seed does not always fall upon stony ground. On his way to inspect a third platoon Captain Wagstaffe passes Bobby Little and his merry men. They are in pairs, indicating targets to one another.

Says Private Walker (oblivious of Captain Wagstaffe's proximity) to his friend, Private McLeary — in an affected parody of his instructor's staccato utterance —

"At yon three Gairman spies, gaun' up a close for tae

52

despatch some wireless telegraphy — fufty roonds — fire!"

To which Private McLeary, not to be outdone, responds —

"Public hoose — in the baur — back o' seeven o'clock — twa drams — fower fingers — rapid!"

*   *   *   *

From this it is a mere step to —

"Butt Pairty, *'shun!* Forrm fourrs! Right! By your left, quick *marrch!"*

— on a bleak and cheerless morning in late October. It is not yet light; but a depressed party of about twenty-five are falling into line at the acrid invitation of two sergeants, who have apparently decided that the pen is mightier than the Lee-Enfield rifle; for each wears one stuck in his glengarry like an eagle's feather, and carries a rabbinical-looking inkhorn slung to his bosom. This literary pose is due to the fact that records are about to be taken of the performances of the Company on the shooting-range.

A half-awakened subaltern, who breakfasted at the grisly hour of quarter-to-six, takes command, and the dolorous procession disappears into the gloom.

Half an hour later the Battalion parades, and sets off, to the sound of music, in pursuit. (It is perhaps needless to state that although we are deficient in rifles, possess neither belts, pouches, nor greatcoats, and are compelled to attach our scanty accoutrements to our persons with ingenious contrivances of string, we boast a fully equipped and highly efficient pipe band, complete with pipers, big drummer, side drummers, and corybantic drum-major.)

By eight o'clock, after a muddy tramp of four miles, we are assembled at the two-hundred-yards firing-point upon Number Three Range. The range itself is little more than a drive cut through a pine-wood. It is nearly half a mile long. Across the far end runs a high sandy embankment, decorated just below the ridge with a row of number-boards — one for each target. Of the targets themselves nothing as yet is to be seen.

"Now then, let's get a move on!" suggests the Senior Captain briskly. "Cockerell, ring up the butts, and ask Captain Wagstaffe to put up the targets."

The alert Mr Cockerell hurries to the telephone, which lives in a small white-painted structure like a gramophone stand. (It has been left at the firing-point by the all-providing butt party.) He turns the call-handle smartly, takes the receiver out of the box, and begins. . . .

There is no need to describe the performance which ensues. All telephone-users are familiar with it. It consists entirely of the word "Hallo!" repeated *crescendo* and *furioso* until exhaustion supervenes.

Presently Mr Cockerell reports to the Captain —

"Telephone out of order, sir."

"I never knew a range telephone that wasn't," replies the Captain, inspecting the instrument. "Still, you might give this one a sporting chance, anyhow. It isn't a *wireless* telephone, you know! Corporal Kemp, connect that telephone for Mr Cockerell."

A marble-faced N.C.O. kneels solemnly upon the turf and raises a small iron trap-door — hitherto overlooked by the omniscient Cockerell — revealing a cavity some six inches deep, containing an electric plughole. Into this he thrusts the terminal of the telephone wire. Cockerell, scarlet in the face, watches him indignantly.

Telephonic communication between firing-point and butts is now established. That is to say, whenever Mr Cockerell rings the bell someone in the butts courteously rings back. Overtures of a more intimate nature are greeted either with stony silence or another fantasia on the bell.

Meanwhile the Captain is superintending firing arrangements.

"Are the first details ready to begin?" he shouts.

"Quite ready, sir," runs the reply down the firing line.

The Captain now comes to the telephone himself. He takes the receiver from Cockerell with masterful assurance.

"Hallo, there!" he calls. "I want to speak to Captain Wagstaffe."

"Honkle yang-yang?" inquires a ghostly voice.

"Captain Wagstaffe! Hurry up!"

Presently the bell rings, and the Captain gets to business.

"That you, Wagstaffe?" he inquires cheerily. "Look here, we're going to fire Practice Seven, Table B — snap-shooting. I want you to raise all the targets for six seconds, just for sighting purposes. Do you understand?"

Here the bell rings continuously for ten seconds. Nothing daunted, the Captain tries again.

"That you, Wagstaffe? Practice Seven, Table B!"

"T'chk, t'chk!" replies Captain Wagstaffe.

"Begin by raising all the targets for six seconds. Then raise them six times for five seconds each — no, as you were! Raise them five times for six seconds each. Got that? I say, are you *there?* What's that?"

Przemysl!" replies the telephone — or something to that effect. "*Czestochowa! Krzyszkowice! Plock!*"

The Captain, now on his mettle, continues —

"I want you to signal the results on the rear targets as the front ones go down. After that we will fire — oh, *curse* the thing!"

He hastily removes the receiver, which is emitting sounds suggestive of the buckling of biscuit-tins, from his ear, and lays it on its rest. The bell promptly begins to ring again.

"Mr Cockerell," he says resignedly, "double up to the butts and ask Captain Wagstaffe —"

"I'm here, old son," replies a gentle voice, as Captain Wagstaffe touches him upon the shoulder. "Been here some time!"

After mutual asperities, it is decided by the two Captains to dispense with the aid of the telephone proper, and communicate by bell alone. Captain Wagstaffe's tall figure strides back across the heather; the red flag on the butts flutters down, and we get to work.

Upon a long row of waterproof sheets — some thirty in all — lie the firers. Beside each is extended the form of a sergeant or officer, tickling his charge's ear with incoherent counsel, and imploring him, almost tearfully, not to get excited.

Suddenly thirty targets spring out of the earth in front of us, only to disappear again just as we have got over our surprise. They are not of the usual bull's-eye pattern, but are what is known as "figure" targets. The lower half is sea-green, the upper, white. In the centre, half on the green and half on the white, is a curious brown smudge. It might be anything, from a splash of mud to one of those mysterious brown-paper patterns which fall out of ladies' papers, but it really is intended to represent the head and shoulders of a man in khaki lying on grass and aiming at us. However, the British private, with his usual genius for misapprehension, has christened this effigy "the beggar in the boat".

With equal suddenness the targets swing up again. Crack! An uncontrolled spirit has loosed off his rifle before it has reached his shoulder. Blistering reproof follows. Then, after three or four seconds, comes a perfect salvo all down the line. The conscientious Mucklewame, slowly raising his foresight as he has been taught to do, from the base of the target to the centre, has just covered the beggar in the boat between wind and water, and is lingering lovingly over the second pull, when the inconsiderate beggar (and his boat) sink unostentatiously into the abyss, leaving the open-mouthed marksman with his finger on the trigger and an unfired cartridge still in the chamber. At the dentist's Time crawls; in snap-shooting contests he sprints.

Another set of targets slide up as the first go down, and upon these the hits are recorded by a forest of black or white discs, waving vigorously in the air. Here and there a red-and-white flag flaps derisively. Muckle-wame gets one of these.

The marking-targets go down to half-mast again, and then comes another tense pause. Then, as the firing-targets reappear, there is another volley. This time Private Mucklewame leads the field, and decapitates a dandelion. The third time he has learned wisdom, and the beggar in the boat gets the bullet where all mocking foes should get it — in the neck!

Snap-shooting over, the combatants retire to the five-hundred-yards firing-point, taking with them that modern hair-shirt, the telephone.

Presently a fresh set of targets swing up — of the bull's-eye variety this time — and the markers are busy once more.

*   *   *   *

The interior of the butts is an unexpectedly spacious place. From the nearest firing-point you would not suspect their existence, except when the targets are up. Imagine a sort of miniature railway station — or rather, half a railway station — sunk into the ground, with a very long platform and a very low roof — eight feet high at the most. Upon the opposite side of this station, instead of the other platform, rises the sandy ridge previously mentioned — the stop-butt — crowned with its row of number-boards. Along the permanent way, in place of sleepers and metals, runs a long and narrow trough, in which, instead of railway carriages, some thirty great iron frames are standing side by side. These frames are double, and hold the targets. They are so arranged that if one is pushed up the other comes down. The markers stand along the platform, like railway porters.

There are two markers to each target. They stand with their backs to the firers, comfortably conscious of several feet of earth and a stout brick wall between them and low shooters. Number one squats down, paste-pot in hand, and repairs the bullet-holes in the unemployed target with patches of black or white paper. Number two, brandishing a pole to which is attached a disc, black on one side and white on the other, is acquiring a permanent crick in the neck through gaping upwards at the target in search of hits. He has to be sharp-eyed, for the bullet-hole is a small one, and springs into existence without any other intimation than a spirt of sand on the bank twenty yards behind. He must be alert, too, and signal the shots as they are made; otherwise the telephone will begin to interest itself on his behalf. The bell will ring, and a sarcastic voice will intimate — assuming that you can hear what it says — that C Company are sending a wreath and message of condolence as their contribution to the funeral of the marker at Number Seven target, who appears to have died at his post within the last ten minutes; coupled with a polite request that his successor may be appointed as rapidly as possible, as the war is not likely to last more than three years. To this the butt-officer replies that C Company had better come a bit closer to the target and try, try again.

There are practically no restrictions as to the length

to which one may go in insulting butt-markers. The Geneva Convention is silent upon the subject, partly because it is almost impossible to say anything which can really hurt a marker's feelings, and partly because the butt-officer always has the last word in any unpleasantness which may arise. That is to say, when defeated over the telephone, he can always lower his targets, and with his myrmidons feign abstraction or insensibility until an overheated subaltern arrives at the double from the five-hundred-yards firing-point, conveying news of surrender.

Captain Wagstaffe was an admitted master of this game. He was a difficult subject to handle, for he was accustomed to return an eye for an eye when repartees were being exchanged; and when overborne by heavier metal — say, a peripatetic "brass-hat" from Hythe — he was accustomed to haul up the red butt-flag (which automatically brings all firing to a standstill), and stroll down the range to refute the intruder at close quarters. We must add that he was a most efficient butt-officer. When he was on duty, markers were most assiduous in their attention to theirs, which is not always the case.

Thomas Atkins rather enjoys marking. For one thing, he is permitted to remove as much clothing as he pleases, and to cover himself with stickiness and grime to his heart's content — always a highly prized privilege. He is also allowed to smoke, to exchange full-flavoured persiflage with his neighbours, and to refresh himself from time to time with mysterious items of provender wrapped in scraps of newspaper. Given an easy-going butt-officer and some timid subalterns, he can spend a very agreeable morning. Even when discipline is strict, marking is preferable to most other fatigues.

Crack! Crack! Crack! The fusilade has begun. Privates Ogg and Hogg are in charge of Number Thirteen target. They are beguiling the tedium of their task by a friendly gamble with the markers on Number Fourteen — Privates Cosh and Tosh. The rules of the game are simplicity itself. After each detail has fired, the target with the higher score receives the sum of one penny from its opponents. At the present moment, after a long run of adversity, Privates Cosh and Tosh are one penny to the good. Once again fortune smiles upon them. The first two shots go right through the bull — eight points straight away. The third is an inner; the fourth another bull; the fifth just grazes the line separating inners and outers. Private Tosh, who is scoring, promptly signals an inner. Meanwhile, target Number Thirteen is also being liberally marked — but by nothing of a remunerative nature. The gentleman at the firing-point is taking what is known as "a fine sight" — so fine, indeed, that each successive bullet either buries itself in the turf fifty yards short, or ricochets joyously from off the bank in front, hurling itself sideways through the target, accompanied by a storm of gravel, and tearing holes therein which even the biassed Ogg cannot class as clean hits.

"We hae gotten eighteen that time," announces Mr Tosh to his rival, swinging his disc and inwardly blessing his unknown benefactor. (For obvious reasons the firer is known only to the marker by a number.) "Hoo's a' wi' you, Jock?"

"There's a [adjective] body here," replies Ogg, with gloomy sarcasm, "flingin' bricks through this yin!" He picks up the red–and–white flag for the fourth time, and unfurls it indignantly to the breeze.

"Here's the officer!" says the warning voice of Hogg. "I doot he'll no allow your last yin, Peter."

He is right. The subaltern in charge of targets Thirteen to Sixteen, after a pained glance at the battered countenance of Number Thirteen, pauses before Fourteen, and jots down a figure on his butt-register.

"Fower, fower, fower, three, three, sirr," announces

Tosh politely.

"Three bulls, one inner, and an ahter, sir," proclaims the Cockney sergeant simultaneously.

"Now, suppose *I* try," suggests the subaltern gently.

He examines the target, promptly disallows Tosh's last inner, and passes on.

"Seventeen *only!*" remarks Private Ogg severely. "I thocht sae!"

Private Cosh speaks — for the first time — removing a paste-brush and some patching-paper from his mouth

"Still, it's better nor a wash-oot! And ony-way, you're due us tippence the noo!"

By way of contrast to the frivolous game of chance in the butts, the proceedings at the firing-point resolve themselves into a desperately earnest test of skill. The fortnight's range-practice is drawing to a close. Each evening registers have been made up, and firing averages adjusted, with the result that A and D Companies are found to have entirely outdistanced B and C, and to be running neck and neck for the championship of the battalion. Up till this morning D's average worked out at something under fifteen (out of a possible twenty), and A's at something over fourteen points. Both are quite amazing and incredible averages for a recruit's course: but then nearly everything about "K(1)" is amazing and incredible. Up till half an hour ago D had, if anything, increased their lead: then dire calamity overtook them.

One Pumpherston, Sergeant-Major and crack shot of the Company, solemnly blows down the barrel of his rifle and prostrates himself majestically upon his more than considerable stomach, for the purpose of firing his five rounds at five hundred yards. His average score so far has been one under "possible". Three officers and a couple of stray corporals gather behind him in eulogistic attitudes.

"How are the Company doing generally, Sergeant-Major?" inquires the Captain of D Company.

"Very well, sir, except for some carelessness," replies the great man impressively. "That man there" — he indicates a shrinking figure hurrying rearwards — "has just spoilt his own score and another man's by putting two shots on the wrong target."

There is a horrified hum at this, for to fire upon someone else's target is the gravest crime in musketry. In the first place, it counts a miss for yourself. In the second, it may do a grievous wrong to your neighbour; for the law ordains that, in the event of more than five shots being found upon any target, only the worst five shall count. Therefore, if your unsolicited contribution takes the form of an outer, it must be counted, to the exclusion, possibly, of a bull. The culprit broke into a double.

Having delivered himself, Sergeant-Major Pumpherston graciously accepted the charger of cartridges which an obsequious acolyte was proffering, rammed it into the magazine, adjusted the sights, spread out his legs to an obtuse angle, and fired his first shot.

All eyes were turned upon target Number Seven. But there was no signal. All the other markers were busy flourishing discs or flags; only Number Seven remained cold and aloof.

The Captain of D Company laughed satirically.

"Number Seven gone to have his hair cut!" he observed.

"Third time this morning, sir," added a sycophantic subaltern.

The Sergeant-Major smiled indulgently.

"I can do without signals, sir," he said. "I know where the shot went all right. I must get the next a *little* more to the left. That last one was a bit too near to three o'clock to be a certainty."

He fired again — with precisely the same result.

Everyone was quite apologetic to the sergeant-major this time.

"This must be stopped," announced the Captain. "Mr Simson, ring up Captain Wagstaffe on the telephone."

But the sergeant-major would not hear of this.

"The butt-registers are good enough for me, sir," he said with a paternal smile. He fired again. Once more the target stared back, blank and unresponsive.

This time the audience were too disgusted to speak. They merely shrugged their shoulders and glanced at one another with sarcastic smiles. The Captain, who had suffered a heavy reverse at the hands of Captain Wagstaffe earlier in the morning, began to rehearse the wording of his address over the telephone.

The sergeant-major fired his last two shots with impressive aplomb — only to be absolutely ignored twice more by Number Seven. Then he rose to his feet and saluted with ostentatious respectfulness.

"Four bulls and one inner, I *think*, sir. I'm afraid I pulled that last one off a bit."

The Captain is already at the telephone. For the moment this most feminine of instruments is found to be in an accommodating frame of mind. Captain Wagstaffe's voice is quickly heard.

"That you, Wagstaffe?" inquires the Captain. "I'm so sorry to bother you, but could you make inquiries and ascertain when the marker on Number Seven is likely to come out of the chloroform?"

"He has been sitting up and taking nourishment for some hours," replies the voice of Wagstaffe. "What message can I deliver to him?"

"None in particular, except that he has not signalled a single one of Sergeant-Major Pumpherston's shots!" replies the Captain of D, with crushing simplicity.

"Half a mo'!" replies Wagstaffe.... Then, presently —

63

"Hallo! Are you there, Whitson?"

"Yes. We are still here," Captain Whitson assures him frigidly.

"Right. Well, I have examined Number Seven target, and there are no shots on it of any kind whatever. But there are ten shots on Number Eight, if that's any help. Buck up with the next lot, will you? We are getting rather bored here. So long!"

There was nothing in it now. D Company had finished. The last two representatives of A were firing, and subalterns with notebooks were performing prodigies of arithmetic. Bobby Little calculated that if these two scored eighteen points each they would pull the Company's total average up to fifteen precisely, beating D by a decimal.

The two slender threads upon which the success of this enterprise hung were named Lindsay and Budge. Lindsay was a phlegmatic youth with watery eyes. Nothing disturbed him, which was fortunate, for the commotion which surrounded him was considerable. A stout sergeant lay beside him on a waterproof sheet, whispering excited counsels of perfection, while Bobby Little danced in the rear, beseeching him to fire upon the proper target.

"Now, Lindsay," said Captain Whitson, in a trembling voice, "you are going to get into a good comfortable position, take your time, and score five bulls."

The amazing part of it all was that Lindsay very nearly did score five bulls. He actually got four, and would have had a fifth had not the stout sergeant, in excess of solicitude, tenderly wiped his watery eye for him with a grubby handkerchief just as he took the first pull for his third shot.

Altogether he scored nineteen; and the gallery, full of congratulations, moved on to inspect the performance of Private Budge, an extremely nervous subject:

who, thanks to the fact that public attention had been concentrated so far upon Lindsay, and that his ministering sergeant was a matter-of-fact individual of few words, had put on two bulls — eight points. He now required to score only nine points in three shots.

Suddenly the hapless youth became aware of the breathless group in his rear. He promptly pulled his trigger, and just flicked the outside edge of the target — two points.

"I doot I'm gettin' a thing nairvous," he muttered apologetically to the sergeant.

"Havers! Shut your heid and give the bull a bash!" responded that admirable person.

The twitching Budge, bracing himself, scored an inner — three points.

"A bull, and we do it!" murmured Bobby Little. Fortunately Budge did not hear.

"Ye're no' daen badly," admitted the sergeant grudgingly.

Budge, a little piqued, determined to do better. He raised his foresight slowly; took the first pull; touched "six o'clock" on the distant bull — luckily the light was perfect — and took the second pull for the last time.

Next moment a white disc rose slowly out of the earth and covered the bull's-eye.

So Bobby Little was able next morning to congratulate his disciples upon being "the best-shooting platoon in the best-shooting Company in the best-shooting Battalion in the Brigade".

Not less that fifty other subalterns within a radius of five miles were saying the same thing to their platoons. It is right to foster a spirit of emulation in young troops.

CHAPTER EIGHT

BILLETS

Scene, a village street deserted. Rain falls. (It has been falling for about three weeks.) A tucket sounds. Enter, reluctantly, soldiery. They grouse. There appear severally, in doorways, children. They stare. And at chamber windows, serving-maids. They make eyes. The soldiery make friendly signs.

SUCH IS THE STAGE setting for our daily morning parade. We have been here for some weeks now, and the populace is getting used to us. But when we first burst upon this peaceful township I think we may say, without undue egoism, that we created a profound sensation. In this sleepy corner of Hampshire His Majesty's uniform, enclosing a casual soldier or sailor on furlough, is a common enough sight, but a whole regiment on the march is the rarest of spectacles. As for this tatterdemalion northern horde, which swept down the street a few Sundays ago, with kilts swinging, bonnets cocked, and pipes skirling, as if they were actually returning from a triumphant campaign instead of only rehearsing for one — well, as I say, the inhabitants had never seen anything like us in the world before. We achieved a *succès fou*. In fact, we were quite embarrassed by the attention bestowed upon us. During our first few parades the audience could with difficulty be kept off the stage. It was impossible to get the children into school, or the maids to come in and make the beds. Whenever a small boy spied an officer, he stood in his way and saluted him. Dogs enlisted in large numbers, sitting down with an air of pleased expectancy in the supernumerary rank, and waiting for this new and delightful pastime to take a fresh turn. When we marched out to our training area, later in the day, infant schools were decanted on to the road under a beaming vicar, to utter what we took to be patriotic sounds and wave handkerchiefs.

Off duty, we fraternised with the inhabitants. The language was a difficulty, of course; but a great deal can be done by mutual goodwill and a few gestures. It would have warmed the heart of a philologist to note the success with which a couple of kilted heroes from the banks of Loch Lomond would sidle up to two giggling damosels of Hampshire at the corner of the High Street, by the post office, and invite them to come for a walk. Though it was obvious that neither party could understand a single word that the other was saying, they never failed to arrive at an understanding; and the quartette, having formed two-deep, would disappear into a gloaming as black as ink, to inhale the evening air and take sweet counsel together — at a temperature of about twenty-five degrees Fahrenheit.

You ought to see us change guard. A similar ceremony takes place, we believe, outside Buckingham Palace every morning, and draws a considerable crowd; but you simply cannot compare it with ours. How often does the guard at Buckingham Palace fix bayonets? Once! and the thing is over. It is hardly worth while turning out to see. *We* sometimes do it as much as seven or eight times before we get it right, and even then we only stop because the sergeant-in-charge is threatened with clergyman's sore throat. The morning Private Mucklewame fixed his bayonet for the first time, two small boys stayed away from school all day in order to see him unfix it when he came off guard in the afternoon. Has anyone ever done that at Buckingham Palace?

However, as I say, they have got used to us now. We fall in for our diurnal labours in comparative solitude, usually in heavy rain and without pomp. We are fairly into the collar by this time. We have been worked desperately hard for more than four months; we are grunting doggedly away at our job, not because we like it, but because we know it is the only thing to do. To march, to dig, to extend, to close; to practise advance-guards and rear-guards, and pickets, in fair weather or foul, often with empty stomachs — that is our daily and sometimes our nightly programme. We are growing more and more efficient, and our powers of endurance are increasing. But, as already stated, we no longer go about our task like singing birds.

It is a quarter to nine in the morning. All down the street doors are opening, and men appear, tugging at their equipment. (Yes, we are partially equipped now.) Most of B Company live in this street. They are fortunate, for only two or three are billeted in each little house, where they are quite domestic pets by this time. Their billeting includes "subsistence", which means that they are catered for by an experienced female instead of a male cooking-class still in the elementary stages of its art.

"A" are not so fortunate. They are living in barns or hay-lofts, sleeping on the floor, eating on the floor, existing on the floor generally. Their food is cooked (by the earnest band of students aforementioned) in open-air camp kitchens; and in this weather it is sometimes difficult to keep the fires alight, and not always possible to kindle them.

"D" are a shade better off. They occupy a large empty mansion at the end of the street. It does not contain a stick of furniture; but there are fireplaces (with

Adam mantelpieces), and the one thing of which the War Office never seems to stint us is coal. So "D" are warm, anyhow. Thirty men live in the drawing-room. Its late tenant would probably be impressed with its new scheme of upholstery. On the floor, straw palliasses and gravy. On the walls, "cigarette photties" — by the way, the children down here call them "fag picters". Across the room run clothes-lines, bearing steaming garments (and tell it not in Gath!) an occasional hare skin.

"C" are billeted in a village two miles away, and we see them but rarely.

The rain has ceased for a brief space — it always does about parade time — and we accordingly fall in. The men are carrying picks and shovels, and make no attempt to look pleased at the circumstance. They realise that they are in for a morning's hard digging, and very likely for an evening's field operations as well. When we began company training a few weeks ago, entrenching was rather popular. More than half of us are miners or tillers of the soil, and the pick and shovel gave us a home-like sensation. Here was a chance, too, of showing regular soldiers how a job should be properly accomplished. So we dug with great enthusiasm.

But A Company have got over that now. They have developed into sufficiently old soldiers to have acquired the correct military attitude towards manual labour. Trench-digging is a "fatigue" to be classed with coal-carrying, floor-scrubbing, and other civilian pursuits. The word "fatigue" is a shibboleth with the British private. Persuade him that a task is part of his duty as a soldier, and he will perform it with tolerable cheerfulness; but once allow him to regard that task as a "fatigue", and he will shirk it whenever possible, and regard himself as a deeply injured individual when called upon to undertake it. Our battalion has now reached a sufficient state of maturity to be constantly on the *qui vive* for cunningly disguised fatigues. The other day, when kilts were issued for the first time, Private Tosh, gloomily surveying his newly unveiled extremities, was heard to remark with a sigh —

"Anither fatigue! Knees tae wash noo!"

Presently Captain Blaikie arrives upon the scene; the senior subaltern reports all present, and we tramp off through the mud to our training area.

We are more or less in possession of our proper equipment now. That is to say, our wearing apparel and the appurtenances thereof are no longer held in position with string. The men have belts, pouches, and slings in which to carry their greatcoats. The greatcoats were the last to materialise. Since their arrival we have lost in decorative effect what we have gained in martial appearance. For a month or two each man wore over his uniform during wet weather — in other words, all day — a garment which the Army Ordnance Department described as "Greatcoat, Civilian, one." An Old Testament writer would have termed it "a coat of many colours." A tailor would have said that it was a "superb vicuna raglan sack." You and I would have called it, quite simply, a reach-me-down. Anyhow, the combined effect was unique. As we plodded patiently along the road in our tarnished finery, with our eye-arresting checks and imitation velvet collars, caked with mud and wrinkled with rain, we looked like nothing so much on earth as a gang of welshers returning from an unsuccessful day at a suburban race-meeting.

But now the khaki-mills have ground out another million yards or so, and we have regulation greatcoats. Water-bottles, haversacks, mess-tins, and waterproof sheets have been slowly filtering into our possession; and whenever we "mobilise", which we do as a rule about once a fortnight — whether owing to invasion scares or as a test of efficiency we do not know — we fall in on our alarm-posts in something distinctly resembling the full "Christmas-tree" rig. Sam Browne belts have been wisely discarded by the officers in favour of web-equipment; and although Bobby Little's shoulders ache with the weight of his pack, he is comfortably conscious of two things — firstly, that even when separated from his baggage he can still subsist in fair comfort on what he carries upon his person; and secondly, that his "expectation of life", as the insurance offices say, has increased about a hundred per cent, now that the German sharpshooters will no longer be able to pick him out from his men.

Presently we approach the scene of our day's work, Area Number Fourteen. We are now far advanced in company training. The barrack square is a thing of the past. Commands are no longer preceded by cautions and explanations. A note on a whistle, followed by a brusque word or gesture, is sufficient to set us smartly on the move.

Suddenly we are called upon to give a test of our quality. A rotund figure upon horseback appears at a bend in the road. Captain Blaikie recognises General Freeman.

(We may note that the General's name is not really Freeman. We are much harried by generals at present. They roam about the country on horseback, and ask company commanders what they are doing; and no company commander has ever yet succeeded in framing an answer which sounds in the least degree credible. There are three generals; we call them Freeman, Hardy, and Willis, because we suspect that they are all — to judge from their fondness for keeping us on the run — financially interested in the consumption of shoe-leather. In other respects they differ, and a wise company commander will carefully bear their idiosyncrasies in mind and act accordingly, if he wishes to be regarded as an intelligent officer.)

Freeman is a man of action. He likes to see people running about. When he appears upon the horizon whole battalions break into a double.

Hardy is one of the old school: he likes things done decently and in order. He worships bright buttons, and exact words of command, and a perfectly wheeling line. He mistrusts unconventional movements and individual tactics. "No use trying to run," he says, "before you can walk." When we see him, we dress the company and advance in review order.

Willis gives little trouble. He seldom criticises, but when he does his criticism is always of a valuable nature; and he is particularly courteous and helpful to young officers. But, like lesser men, he has his fads. These are two — feet and cookery. He has been known to call a private out of the ranks on a route-march and request him to take his boots off for purposes of public display. "A soldier marches on two things," he announces — "his feet and his stomach." Then he calls up another man and asks him if he knows how to make a sea-pie. The man never does know, which is fortunate, for otherwise General Willis would not be able to tell him. After that he trots happily away, to ask someone else.

However, here we are face to face with General Freeman. Immediate action is called for. Captain Blaikie flings an order over his shoulder to the subaltern in command of the leading platoon —

"Pass back word that this road is under shell fire. Move!"

— and rides forward to meet the General.

In ten seconds the road behind him is absolutely clear, and the men are streaming out to right and left in half-platoons. Waddell's platoon has the hardest time, for they were passing a quickset hedge when the order came. However, they hurl themselves blasphemously through, and double on, scratched and panting.

"Good morning, sir!" says Captain Blaikie, saluting.

"Good morning!" says General Freeman. "What was that last movement?"

"The men are taking 'artillery' formation, sir. I have just passed the word down that the road is under shell fire."

"Quite so. But don't you think you ought to keep some of your company in rear, as a supporting line? I see you have got them all up on one front."

By this time A Company is advancing in its original direction, but split up into eight half-platoons in single file — four on each side of the road, at intervals of thirty yards. The movement has been quite smartly carried out. Still, a critic must criticise or go out of business. However, Captain Blaikie is an old hand.

"I was assuming that my company formed part of a battalion, sir," he explained. "There are supposed to be three other companies in rear of mine."

"I see. Still, tell two of your sections to fall back and form a supporting line."

Captain Blaikie, remembering that generals have little time for study of such works as the new drill-book, and that when General Freeman says "section" he probably means "platoon", orders Numbers Two and Four to fall back. This manoeuvre is safely accomplished.

"Now, let me see them close on the road."

Captain Blaikie blows a whistle, and slaps himself on the top of the head. In three minutes the long-suffering platoons are back on the road, extracting thorns from their flesh and assuaging the agony of their abrasions by clandestine massage.

General Freeman rides away, and the column moves on. Two minutes later Captain Wagstaffe doubles up from the rear to announce that General Hardy is only two hundred yards behind.

"Pass back word to the men," groans Captain

Blaikie, "to march at attention, put their caps straight, and slope their shovels properly. And send an orderly to that hill-top to look out for General Willis. Tell him to unlace his boots when he gets there, and on no account to admit that he knows how to make a sea-pie!"

CHAPTER NINE

MID-CHANNEL

THE GREAT WAR has been terribly hard on the text-books.

When we began to dig trenches, many weeks ago, we always selected a site with a good field of fire.

"No good putting your trenches," said the text-book, "where you can't see the enemy."

This seemed only common-sense; so we dug our trenches in open plains, or on the forward slope of a hill, where we could command the enemy's movements up to two thousand yards.

Another maxim which we were urged to take to heart was — When not entrenched, always take advantage of *natural* cover of any kind; such as farm buildings, plantations, and railway embankments.

We were also given practice in describing and recognising inconspicuous targets at long range, in order to be able to harass the enemy the moment he showed himself.

Well, recently generals and staff officers have been coming home from the front and giving us lectures. We regard most lectures as a "fatigue" — but not these. We have learned more from these quiet-mannered, tired-looking men in a brief hour than from all the manuals that ever came out of Gale and Polden's. We have heard the history of the War from the inside. We know why our Army retreated from Mons; we know what prevented the relief of Antwerp. But above all, we have learned to revise some of our most cherished theories.

Briefly, the amended version of the law and the prophets comes to this:—

Never, under any circumstances, place your trenches where you can see the enemy a long way off. If you do, he will inevitably see you too, and will shell you out of them in no time. You need not be afraid of being rushed; a field of fire of two hundred yards or so will be sufficient to wipe him off the face of the earth.

Never, under any circumstances, take cover in farm buildings, or plantations, or behind railway embankments, or in any place likely to marked on a large-scale map. Their position and range are known to a yard. Your safest place is the middle of an open plain or ploughed field. There it will be more difficult for the enemy's range-takers to gauge your exact distance.

In musketry, concentrate all your energies on taking care of your rifle and practising "rapid". You will seldom have to fire over a greater distance than two hundred yards; and at that range British rapid fire is the most dreadful medium of destruction yet devised in warfare.

All this scraps a good deal of laboriously acquired learning, but it rings true. So we site our trenches now according to the lessons taught us by the bitter experience of others.

Having arrived at our alloted area, we get to work. The firing-trench proper is outlined on the turf a hundred yards or so down the reverse slope of a low hill. When it is finished it will be a mere crack in the ground, with no front cover to speak of; for that would make it conspicuous. Number One Platoon gets to work on this. To Number Two is assigned a more subtle task — namely, the construction of a dummy trench a comfortable distance ahead, dug out to the depth of a few inches, to delude inquisitive aeroplanes, and rendered easily visible to the enemy's observing stations by a parapet of newly-turned earth. Numbers Three and Four concentrate their energies upon the supporting trench and its approaches.

The firing-trench is our place of business — our office in the city, so to speak. The supporting trench is our suburban residence, whither the weary toiler may betake himself periodically (or, more correctly, in relays) for purposes of refreshment and repose. The firing-trench, like most business premises, is severe in design and destitute of ornament. But the suburban trench lends itself to more imaginative treatment. An auctioneer's catalogue would describe it as *A commodious bijou residence, on* (or of) *chalky soil; three feet wide and six feet deep; in the style of the best troglodyte period. Thirty seconds brisk crawl (or per stretcher) from the firing line. Gas laid on* —

But only once, in a field near Aldershot, where Private Mucklewame first laid bare, and then perforated, the town main with his pick.

— *With own water supply* — ankle-deep at times — *telephone, and the usual offices.*

We may note that the telephone communicates with the observing-station, lying well forward, in line with the dummy trench. The most important of the usual offices is the hospital — a cavern excavated at the back of the trench, and roofed over with hurdles, earth and turf.

It is hardly necessary to add that we do not possess a real field-telephone. But when you have spent four months in firing dummy cartridges, performing bayonet exercises without bayonets, taking hasty cover from non-existent shell fire, capturing positions held by no enemy, and enacting the part of a "casualty" without having received a scratch, telephoning without a telephone is a comparatively simple operation.

All you require is a ball of string and no sense of humour. Second Lieutenant Waddell manages our telephone.

Meanwhile we possess our souls in patience. We know that the factories are humming night and day on our behalf; and that if, upon a certain day in a certain month, the contractors do not deliver our equipment down to the last water-bottle cork, "K" will want to know the reason why; and we cannot imagine any contractor being so foolhardy as to provoke that terrible man into an inquiring attitude of mind.

Now we are at work. We almost wish that Freeman, Hardy, and Willis could see us. Our buttons may occasionally lack lustre; we may cherish unorthodox notions as to the correct method of presenting arms; we may not always present an unbroken front on the parade-ground — but we *can* dig! Even the fact that we do not want to, cannot altogether eradicate a truly human desire to "show off". "Each man to his art", we say. We are quite content to excel in ours, the oldest in the world. We know enough now about the conditions of the present war to be aware that when we go out on service only three things will really count — to march; to dig; and to fire, upon occasion, fifteen rounds a minute. Our rapid fire is already fair; we can march more than a little; and if men who have been excavating the bowels of the earth for eight hours a day ever since they were old enough to swing a pick cannot make short work of a Hampshire chalk down, they are no true members of their Trades Union or the First Hundred Thousand.

We have stuck to the phraseology of our old calling.

"Whaur's ma drawer?" inquires Private Hogg, a thick-set young man with bandy legs, wiping his countenance with a much-tattooed arm. He has just completed five strenuous minutes with a pick. "Come away, Geordie, wi' yon shovel!"

The shovel is preceded by an adjective. It is the only

adjective that A Company knows. (No, not that one. The second on the list!)

Mr George Ogg steps down into the breach, and sets to work. He is a small man, strongly resembling the Emperor of China in a third-rate provincial pantomime. His weapon is the spade. In civil life he would have shovelled the broken coal into a "hutch" and "hurled" it away to the shaft. That was why Private Hogg referred to him as a "drawer". In his military capacity he now removes the chalky soil from the trench with great dexterity, and builds it up into a neat parapet behind, as a precaution against the back-blast of a "Black Maria".

There are not enough picks and shovels to go round — *cela va sans dire.* However, Private Mucklewame and others, who are not of the delving persuasion, exhibit no resentment. Digging is not their department. If you hand them a pick and shovel and invite them to set to work, they lay the pick upon the ground beside the trench and proceed to shovel earth over it until they have lost it. At a later stage in this great war-game they will fight for these picks and shovels like wild beasts. Shrapnel is a sure solvent of professional etiquette.

However, today the pickless squad are lined up a short distance away by the relentless Captain Wagstaffe, and informed —

"You are under fire from that wood. Dig yourselves in!"

Digging oneself in is another highly unpopular fatigue. First of all you produce your portable entrenching-tool — it looks like a combination of a modern tack-hammer and a medieval back-scratcher — and fit it to its haft. Then you lie flat upon your face on the wet grass, and having scratched up some small lumps of turf, proceed to build these into a parapet. Into the hole formed by the excavation of the turf you then put your head, and in this ostrich-like posture

79

await further instructions. Private Mucklewame is of the opinion that it would be equally effective, and infinitely less fatiguing, simply to lie down prone and close the eyes.

After Captain Wagstaffe has criticised the preliminary parapets — most of them are condemned as not being bullet-proof — the work is continued. It is not easy, and never comfortable, to dig lying down; but we must all learn to do it; so we proceed painfully to construct a shallow trough for our bodies and an annexe for our boots. Gradually we sink out of sight, and Captain Wagstaffe, standing fifty yards to our front, is able to assure us that he can now see nothing — except Private Mucklewame's lower dorsal curve.

By this time the rain has returned for good, and the short winter day is drawing to a gloomy close. It is after three, and we have been working, with one brief interval, for nearly five hours. The signal is given to take shelter. We huddle together under the leafless trees, and get wetter.

Next comes the order to unroll greatcoats. Five minutes later comes another — to fall in. Tools are counted; there is the usual maddening wait while the search is made for a missing pick. But at last the final word of command rings out, and the sodden, leaden-footed procession sets out on its four-mile tramp home.

We are not in good spirits. One's frame of mind at all times depends largely upon what the immediate future has to offer; and, frankly, we have little to inspire us in that direction at present. When we joined, four long months ago, there loomed largely and splendidly before our eyes only two alternatives — victory in battle or death with honour. We might live, or we might die; but life, while it lasted, would not lack great moments. In our haste we had overlooked the long dreary waste which lay — which always lies — between dream and fulfilment. The glorious splash of patriotic fervour which launched us on our way has subsided; we have reached mid-channel; and the haven where we would be is still afar off. The brave future of which we have dreamed in our dour and uncommunicative souls seems as remote as ever, and the present has settled down into a permanency.

Today, for instance, we have tramped a certain number of miles; we have worked for a certain number of hours; and we have got wet through for the hundredth time. We are now tramping home to a dinner which will probably not be ready, because, as yesterday, it has been cooked in the open air under weeping skies. While waiting for it, we shall clean the same old rifle. When night falls, we shall sleep uneasily upon a comfortless floor, in an atmosphere of stale food and damp humanity. In the morning we shall rise up reluctantly, and go forth, probably in heavy rain, to our labour until the evening — the same labour and the same evening. We admit that it can't be helped: the officers and the authorities do their best for us under discouraging circumstances: but there it is. Out at the front, we hear, men actually get as much as three days off at a time — three days of hot baths, and abundant food and dry beds. To us, in our present frame of mind, that seems worth any number of bullets and frostbites.

And — bitterest thought of all — New Year's Day, with all its convivial associations, is only a few weeks away. When it comes, the folk at home will celebrate it, doubtless with many a kindly toast to the lads "oot there", and the lads "doon there". But what will that profit us? In this barbarous country we understand that they take no notice of the sacred festival at all. There will probably be a route-march, to keep us out of the public-houses.

Et patiti, et patita. Are we fed up? Yes!

As we swing down the village street, slightly cheered by a faint aroma of Irish stew — the cooks have got the fires alight after all — the adjutant rides up, and reins in his horse beside our company commander.

Battalion orders of some kind! Probably a full-dress parade, to trace a missing bayonet!

Presently he rides away; and Captain Blaikie, instead of halting and dismissing us in the street as usual, leads us down an alley into the back-yard which serves as our apology for a parade-ground. We form close column of platoons, stand at ease, and wait resignedly.

Then Captain Blaikie's voice falls upon our ears.

"A Company, I have an announcement to make to you. His Majesty the King —"

So that is it. Another Royal Review! Well, it will be a break in the general monotony.

"— who has noted your hard work, good discipline, and steady progress with the keenest satisfaction and pride —"

We are not utterly forgotten, then.

"— has commanded that every man in the battalion is to have seven days' full leave of absence."

"A-a-ah!" We strain our tingling ears.

"We are to go by companies, a week at a time. 'C' will go first."

"C indeed! Who are C, to — ?"

"A Company's leave — *our* leave — will begin on the twenty-eighth of December, and extend to the third of January."

The staccato words sink slowly in, and then thoughts come tumbling.

"Free — free on New Year's Day! Almichty! Free to gang hame! Free tae —"

Then comes an icy chill upon our hearts. How are we to get home? Scotland is hundreds of miles away. The fare, even on a "soldier's" ticket —

But the Captain has not quite finished.

"Every man will receive a week's pay in advance; and his fare, home and back, will be paid by Government. That is all."

And quite enough too! We rock upon our squelching feet. But the Captain adds, without any suspicion of his parade-ground manner —

"If I may say so, I think that if ever men deserved a good holiday, you do. Company, slope arms! Dis — *miss!*"

We do not cheer: we are not built that way. But as we stream off to our Irish stew, the dourest of us says in his heart —

"God save the King!"

CHAPTER TEN

DEEDS OF DARKNESS

A MOONLIGHT, WINTRY NIGHT. Four hundred men are clumping along the frost-bound road, under the pleasing illusion that because they are neither whistling nor talking they are making no noise.

At the head of the column march Captains Mackintosh and Shand, the respective commanders of C and D Companies. Occasionally Mackintosh, the senior, interpolates a remark of casual or professional nature. To all these his colleague replies in a low and reproachful whisper. The pair represent two schools of military thought — a fact of which their respective subalterns are well aware — and act accordingly.

"In preparing troops for active service, you must make the conditions as *real* as possible from the very outset," postulates Shand. "Perform all your exercises just as you would in war. When you dig trenches, let every man work with his weather-eye open and his rifle handy, in case of sudden attack. If you go out on night operations don't advertise your position by stopping to give your men a recitation. No talking — no smoking — no unnecessary delay or exposure! Just go straight to your point of deployment, and do what you came out to do."

To this Mackintosh replies —

"That's all right for trained troops. But ours aren't half-trained yet; all our work just now is purely educational. It's no use expecting a gang of rivet-heaters from Clydebank to form an elaborate outpost line, just because you whispered a few sweet nothings in the dark to your leading section of fours! You simply *must* explain every step you take, at present."

But Shand shakes his head.

"It's not soldierly," he sighs.

Hence the present one-sided — or apparently one-sided — dialogue. To the men marching immediately behind, it sounds like something between a soliloquy and a chat over the telephone.

Presently Captain Mackintosh announces —

"We might send the scouts ahead now, I think."

Shand gives an inaudible assent. The column is halted, and the scouts called up. A brief command, and they disappear into the darkness, at the double. C and D Companies give them five minutes' start, and move on. The road at this point runs past a low mossy wall, surmounted by a venerable yew hedge, clipped at intervals into the semblance of some heraldic monster. Beyond the hedge, in the middle distance, looms a square and stately Georgian mansion, whose lights twinkle hospitably.

"I think, Shand," suggests Mackintosh with more formality, now that he is approaching the scene of action, "that we might attack at two different points, each of us with his own company. What is your opinion?"

The officer addressed makes no immediate reply. His gaze is fixed upon the yew hedge, as if searching for gun positions or vulnerable points. Presently, however, he turns away, and coming close to Captain Mackintosh, put his lips to his left ear. Mackintosh prepares his intellect for the reception of a pearl of strategy.

But Captain Shand merely announces, in his regulation whisper —

"Dam pretty girl lives in that house, old man!"

*   *   *   *

Private Peter Dunshie, scout, groping painfully and profanely through a close-growing wood, paused to unwind a clinging tendril from his bare knees. As he bent down, his face came into sudden contact with a cold, wet, prickly bramblebush, which promptly drew a loving but excoriating finger across his right cheek.

He started back, with a muffled exclamation. Instantly there arose at his very feet the sound as of a motor-engine being wound up, and a flustered and protesting cock-pheasant hoisted itself tumultuously clear of the undergrowth and sailed away, shrieking, over the trees.

Finally, a hare, which had sat cowering in the bracken, hare-like, when it might have lopped away, selected this, the one moment when it ought to have sat still, to bolt frantically between Peter's bandy legs and speed away down a long moon-dappled avenue.

Private Dunshie, a prey to nervous shock, said what naturally rose to his lips. To be frank, he said it several times. He had spent the greater part of his life selling evening papers in the streets of Glasgow: and the profession of journalism, though it breeds many virtues in its votaries, is entirely useless as a preparation for conditions either of silence or solitude. Private Dunshie had no experience of either of these things, and consequently feared them both. He was actually afraid. What he understood and appreciated was Argyle Street on a Saturday night. That was life! That was light! That was civilisation! As for creeping about in this uncanny wood, filled with noxious animals and adhesive vegetation — well, Dunshie was heartily sorry that he had ever volunteered for service as a scout. He had only done so, of course, because the post seemed to offer certain relaxations from the austerity of company routine — a little more freedom of movement, a little less trench-digging, and a minimum of supervision. He would have been thankful for a supervisor now!

That evening, when the scouts doubled ahead, Lieutenant Simson had halted them upon the skirts of a dark, dreich plantation, and said —

"A and B Companies represent the enemy. They are beyond that crest, finishing the trenches which were begun the other day. They intend to hold these against our attack. Our only chance is to take them by surprise. As they will probably have thrown out a line of outposts, you scouts will now scatter and endeavour to get through that line, or at least obtain exact knowledge of its composition. My belief is that the enemy will content themselves with placing a piquet on each of the two roads which run through their position; but it is possible that they will also post sentry-groups in the wood which lies between. However, that is what you have to find out. Don't go and get captured. Move!"

The scouts silently scattered, and each man set out to pierce his allotted section of the enemy's position. Private Dunshie, who had hoped for a road, or at least a cart-track, to follow, found himself, by the worst of luck, assigned to a portion of the thick belt of wood which stretched between the two roads. Nature had not intended him for a pioneer: he was essentially a city man. However, he toiled on, rending the undergrowth, putting up game, falling over tree-roots, and generally acting as advertising agent for the approaching attack.

By way of contrast, two hundred yards to his right, picking his way with cat-like care and rare enjoyment, was Private McSnape. He was of the true scout breed. In the dim and distant days before the call of the blood had swept him into K (1), he had been a Boy Scout of no mean repute. He was clean in person and courteous in manner. He could be trusted to deliver a message promptly. He could light a fire in a high wind with two matches, and provide himself with a meal of sorts where another would have starved. He could distinguish an oak from an elm, and was sufficiently familiar with the movements of the heavenly bodies to be able to find his way across country by night. He was truthful, and amenable to discipline. In short, he was the embodiment of a system which in times of peace had served as a text for innumerable well-meaning but muddle-headed politicians of a certain type, who made a speciality of keeping the nation upon the alert against the insidious encroachments of — Heaven help us! — Militarism!

Tonight all McSnape's soul was set on getting through the enemy's outpost line, and discovering a way of ingress for the host behind him. He had no map, but he had the Plough and a fitful moon to guide him, and he held a clear notion of the disposition of the trenches in his retentive brain. On his left he could hear the distressing sounds of Dunshie's dolorous progress; but these were growing fainter. The reason was that Dunshie, like most persons who follow the line of least resistance, was walking in a circle. In fact, a few minutes later his circuitous path brought him out upon the long straight road which ran up over the hill towards the trenches.

With a sigh of relief Dunshie stepped out upon the good hard macadam, and proceeded with the merest show of stealth up the gentle gradient. But he was not yet at ease. The over-arching trees formed a tunnel in which his footsteps reverberated uncomfortably. The moon had retired behind a cloud. Dunshie, gregarious and urban, quaked anew. Reflecting longingly upon his bright and cosy billet with the "subsistence" which was doubtless being prepared against his return, he saw no occasion to reconsider his opinion that in the country no decent body should ever be called up to go out after dark unaccompanied. At that moment Dunshie would have bartered his soul for the sight of an electric tram.

The darkness grew more intense. Something stirred in the wood beside him, and his skin tingled. An owl hooted suddenly, and he jumped. Next, the gross darkness was illuminated by a pale and ghostly radiance, coming up from behind; and something brushed past him — something which squeaked and panted. His hair rose upon his scalp. A friendly "Good-night!" uttered in a strong Hampshire accent into his left ear, accentuated rather than soothed his terrors. He sat down suddenly upon a bank by the roadside, and feebly mopped his moist brow.

The bicycle, having passed him, wobbled on up the hill, shedding a fitful ray upon alternate sides of the road. Suddenly — raucous and stunning, but oh, how sweet! — rang out the voice of Dunshie's lifelong friend, Private Mucklewame.

"Halt! Wha goes there?"

The cyclist made no reply, but kept his devious course. Private Mucklewame, who liked to do things decently and in order, stepped heavily out of the hedge into the middle of the road, and repeated his question in a reproving voice. There was no answer.

This was most irregular. According to the text of the spirited little dialogue in which Mucklewame had been recently rehearsed by his piquet commander, the man on the bicycle ought to have said "Friend!" This cue received, Mucklewame was prepared to continue. Without it he was gravelled. He tried once more.

"Halt! Wha goes —"

"On His Majesty's Service, my lad!" responded a

hearty voice; and the postman, supplementing this information with a friendly good-night, wobbled up the hill and disappeared from sight.

The punctilious Mucklewame was still glaring severely after this unseemly "gagger", when he became aware of footsteps upon the road. A pedestrian was plodding up the hill in the wake of the postman. He would stand no nonsense this time.

"Halt!" he commanded. "Wha goes there?"

"Hey, Jock," inquired a husky voice, "is that you?"

This was another most irregular answer. Declining to be drawn into impromptu irrelevancies, Mucklewame stuck to his text.

"Advance yin," he continued, "and give the coontersign, if any!"

Private Dunshie drew nearer.

"Jock," he inquired wistfully, "hae ye gotten a fag?"

"Aye," replied Mucklewame, friendship getting the better of conscience.

"Wull ye give a body yin?"

"Aye. But ye canna smoke on ootpost duty," explained Mucklewame sternly. "Forbye, the officer has no' been roond yet," he added.

"Onyway," urged Dunshie eagerly, "let me be your prisoner! Let me bide with the other boys in here ahint the dyke!"

The hospitable Mucklewame agreed, and Scout Dunshie, overjoyed at the prospect of human companionship, promptly climbed over the low wall and attached himself, in the *rôle* of languishing captive, to Number Two Sentry-Group of Number Three Piquet.

*   *   *   *

Meanwhile McSnape had reached the forward edge of the wood, and was cautiously reconnoitring the open ground in front of him. The moon had disappeared altogether now, but McSnape was able to calculate, by reason of the misdirected exuberance of the vigilant Mucklewame, the exact position of the sentry-group on the left-hand road. About the road on his right he was not so certain; so he set out cautiously towards it, keeping to the edge of the wood, and pausing every few yards to listen. There must be a sentry-group some-where here, he calculated — say midway between the roads. He must walk warily.

Easier said than done. At this very moment a twig snapped beneath his foot with a noise like a pistol-shot, and a covey of partridges, lying out upon the stubble beside him, made an indignant evacuation of their bedroom. The mishap seemed fatal: McSnape stood like a stone. But no alarm followed, and presently all was still again — so still, indeed, that presently, out on the right, two hundred yards away, McSnape heard a man cough and then spit. Another sentry was located!

Having decided that there was no sentry-group be-tween the two roads, McSnape turned his back upon the wood and proceeded cautiously forward. He was not quite satisfied in his mind about things. He knew that Captain Wagstaffe was in command of this sec-tion of the defence. He cherished a wholesome respect for that efficient officer, and doubted very much if he would really leave so much of his front entirely unguarded.

Next moment the solution of the puzzle was in his very hand — in the form of a stout cord stretching from right to left. He was just in time to avoid tripping over it. It was suspended about six inches above the ground.

You cannot follow a clue in two directions at once; so after a little consideration McSnape turned and crawled along to his right, being careful to avoid touching the cord. Presently a black mass loomed before him, acting apparently as terminus to the cord. Lying flat on his stomach, in order to get as much as possible of this obstacle between his eyes and the sky, McSnape was presently able to descry, plainly silhouetted against the starry landscape, the profile of one Bain, a scout of A Company, leaning comfortably against a small bush, and presumably holding the end of the cord in his hand.

McSnape wriggled silently away, and paused to reflect. Then he began to creep forward once more.

Having covered fifty yards, he turned to his right again, and presently found himself exactly between Bain and the trenches. As he expected, his hand now descended upon another cord, lying loosely on the ground, and running at right angles to the first. Plainly Bain was holding one end of this, and some one in the trenches — Captain Wagstaffe himself, as like as not — was holding the other. If an enemy stumbled over the trip-cord, Bain would warn the defence by twitching the alarm-cord.

Five minutes later McSnape was back at the rendezvous, describing to Simson what he had seen. That wise subaltern promptly conducted him to Captain Mackintosh, who was waiting with his Company for something to go upon. Shand had departed with his own following to make an independent attack on the right flank. Seven of the twelve scouts were there. Of the missing, Dunshie, as we know, was sunning his lonely soul in the society of his foes; two had lost themselves, and the remaining two had been captured by a reconnoitring patrol. Of the seven which strayed not, four had discovered the trip-cord; so it was evident that that ingenious contrivance extended along the whole line. Only McSnape, however, had penetrated farther. The general report was that the position was closely guarded from end to end.

"You say you found a cord running back from Bain to the trenches, McSnape," asked Captain Mackintosh, "and a sentry holding on to it?"

"Yess, sirr," replied the scout, standing stiffly to attention in the dark.

"If we could creep out of the wood and rush *him*, we might be able to slip our attack in at that point," said the Captain. "You say there is cover to within twenty yards of where he is sitting?"

"Yes, sirr."

"Still, I'm afraid he'll pull that cord a bit too soon for us."

"He'll no, sirr," remarked McSnape confidently.

"Why not?" asked the Captain.

McSnape told him.

Captain Mackintosh surveyed the small wizened figure before him almost affectionately.

"McSnape," he said, "tomorrow I shall send in your name for lance-corporal!"

*   *   *   *

The defenders were ready. The trenches were finished: "A" and "B" had adjusted their elbow-rests to their liking, and blank ammunition had been served out. Orders upon the subject of firing were strict.

"We won't loose off a single shot until we actually *see* you," Captain Blaikie had said to Captain Mackintosh. "That will teach your men to crawl upon their little tummies, and ours to keep their eyes skinned."

(Captain Wagstaffe's string alarm had been an afterthought. At least, it was not mentioned to the commander of the attack.)

Orders were given that the men were to take things easily for half an hour or so, as the attack could not possibly be developed within that time. The officers established themselves in a splinter-proof shelter at the back of the supporting trench, and partook of provender from their haversacks.

"I don't suppose they'll attack much before nine,"

said the voice of a stout major named Kemp. "My word, it is dark in here! *And* dull! Curse the Kaiser!"

"I don't know," said Wagstaffe thoughtfully. "War is hell, and all that, but it has a good deal to recommend it. I wipes out all the small nuisances of peace-time."

"Such as —"

"Well, Suffragettes, and Futurism, and — and —"

"Bernard Shaw," suggested another voice. "Hall Caine —"

"Yes, and the Tango, and party politics, and golf-maniacs. Life and Death, and the things that really are big, get viewed in their proper perspective for once in a way."

"And look how the War has bucked up the nation," said Bobby Little, all on fire at once. "Look at the way girls have given up fussing over clothes and things, and taken to nursing."

"My poor young friend," said the voice of the middle-aged Kemp, "tell me honestly, would you like to be attended to by some of the young women who have recently taken up the nursing profession?"

"Rather!" said Bobby, with thoughtless fervour.

"I didn't say *one*," Kemp pointed out, amid laughter, "but *some*. Of course we all know of one. Even I do. It's the rule, not the exception, that we are dealing with just now."

Bobby, realising that he had been unfairly surprised in a secret, felt glad that the darkness covered his blushes.

"Well, take my tip," continued Kemp, "and avoid amateur ministering angels, my son. I studied the species in South Africa. For twenty-four hours they nurse you to death, and after that they leave you to perish of starvation. Women in war-time are best left at home."

A youthful paladin in the gloom timidly mentioned the name of Florence Nightingale.

"One Nightingale doesn't make a base hospital,"

replied Kemp. "I take off my hat — we all do — to women who are willing to undergo the drudgery and discomfort which hospital training involves. But I'm not talking about Florence Nightingales. The young person whom I am referring to is just intelligent enough to understand that the only possible thing to do this season is to nurse. She qualifies herself for her new profession by dressing up like one of the chorus of *The Quaker Girl,* and getting her portrait, thus attired, into *The Tatler.* Having achieved this, she has graduated. She then proceeds to invade any hospital that is available, where she flirts with everything in pyjamas, and freezes you with a look if you ask her to empty a basin or change your sheets. I know her! I've had some, and I know her! She is one of the minor horrors of war. In peace-time she goes out on Alexandra Day, and stands on the steps of men's clubs and pesters the members to let her put a rose in their button-holes. What such a girl wants is a good old-fashioned mother who knows how to put a slipper to its right use!"

"I don't think," observed Wagstaffe, since Kemp had apparently concluded his philippic, "that young girls are the only people who lose their heads. Consider all the poisonous young blighters that one sees about town just now. Their uplift is enormous, and their manners in public horrid; and they hardly know enough about their new job to stand at attention when they hear *God Save the King.* In fact, they deserve to be nursed by your little friends, Bobby!"

"They are all that you say," conceded Kemp. "But after all, they do have a fairly stiff time of it on duty, and they are going to have a much stiffer time later on. And they are not going to back out when the romance of the new uniform wears off, remember. Now these girls will play the angel-of-mercy game for a week or two, and then jack up and confine their efforts to getting hold of a wounded officer and taking him to the theatre. It is *dernier cri* to take a wounded officer about with you at present. Wounded officers have quite superseded Pekinese, I am told."

"Women certainly are the most extraordinary creatures," mused Ayling, a platoon commander of "B". "In private life I am a beak at a public school —"

"What school?" inquired several voices. Ayling gave the name, found that there were two of the school's old boys present, and continued —

"Just as I was leaving to join this battalion, the Head received a letter from a boy's mother intimating that she was obliged to withdraw her son, as he had received a commission in the army for the duration of the war. She wanted to know if the Head would keep her son's place open for him until he came back! What do you think of that?"

"Sense of proportion wasn't invented when women were made," commented Kemp. "But we are wandering from the subject, which is: what advantages are we, personally, deriving from the war? Wagger, what are you getting out of it?"

"Half-a-crown a day extra pay as Assistant Adjutant," replied Wagstaffe laconically. "Ainslie, wake up and tell us what the war has done for you, since you abandoned the Stock Exchange and took to foot-slogging."

"Certainly," replied Ainslie. "A year ago I spent my days trying to digest my food, and my nights trying to sleep. I was not at all successful in either enterprise. I can now sit down to a supper of roast pork and bottled stout, go to bed directly afterwards, sleep all night, and wake up in the morning without thinking unkind things of anybody — not even my relations-in-law! Bless the Kaiser, say I! Borrodaile, what about you? Any complaints?"

"Thank you," replied Borrodaile's dry voice; "there are no complaints. In civil life I am what is known as a 'prospective candidate'. For several years I have been exercising this, the only method of advertising permitted to a barrister, by nursing a constituency. That is, I go down to the country once a week, and there reduce myself to speechlessness soliciting the votes of the people who put my opponent in twenty years ago, and will keep him in by a two thousand majority as long as he cares to stand. I have been at it five years, but so far the old gentleman has never so much as betrayed any knowledge of my existence."

"That must be rather galling," said Wagstaffe.

"Ah! but listen! Of course party politics have now been merged in the common cause — see local organs, *passim* — and both sides are working shoulder to shoulder for the maintenance of our national existence."

"*Applause!*" murmured Kemp.

"That is to say," continued Borrodaile with calm relish, "my opponent, whose strong suit for the last twenty years has been to cry down the horrors of militarism, and the madness of national service, and the unwieldy size of the British Empire, is now compelled to spend his evenings taking the chair at mass meetings for the encouragement of recruiting. I believe the way in which he eats up his own previous utterances on the subject is quite superb. On these occasions I always send him a telegram, containing a kindly pat on the back for him and a sort of semi-official message for the audience. He has to read this out on the platform!"

"What sort of message?" asked a delighted voice.

"Oh — *Send along some more of our boys. Lord Kitchener says there are none to touch them. Borrodaile, Bruce and Wallace Highlanders.* Or — *All success to the meeting, and best thanks to you personally for carrying on in my absence. Borrodaile, Bruce and Wallace Highlanders.* I have a lot of quiet fun," said Borrodaile meditatively, "composing those telegrams. I rather fancy" — he examined the luminous watch on his wrist — "yes, it's five minutes past eight: I rather fancy the old thing is reading one now!"

The prospective candidate leaned back against the damp wall of the dug-out with a happy sigh. "What have you got out of the war, Ayling?" he inquired.

"Change," said Ayling.

"For better or worse?"

"If you had spent seven years in a big public school," said Ayling, "teaching exactly the same thing, at exactly the same hour, to exactly the same kind of boy, for weeks on end, what sort of change would you welcome most?"

"Death," said several voices.

"Nothing of the kind!" said Ayling warmly. "It's a great life, if you are cut out for it. But there is no doubt that the regularity of the hours, and the absolute certainty of the future, make a man a bit groovy. Now in this life we are living we have to do lots of dull or unpleasant things, but they are never quite the same things. They are progressive, and not circular, if you know what I mean; and the immediate future is absolutely unknown, which is an untold blessing. What about you, Sketchley?"

A fat voice replied —

"War is good for adipose Special Reservists. I have decreased four inches round the waist since October. Next?"

So the talk ran on. Young Lochgair, heir to untold acres in the far north and master of unlimited pocket-money, admitted frankly that the sum of eight-and-sixpence per day, which he was now earning by the sweat of his brow and the expenditure of shoe-leather, was sweeter to him than honey in the honeycomb. Hattrick, who had recently put up a plate in Harley Street, said it was good to be earning a living wage at last. Mr Waddell, pressed to say a few words in encouragement of the present campaign, delivered himself of a guarded but illuminating eulogy of war as a cure for indecision of mind; from which, coupled with a coy reference to "some one" in distant St Andrews, the company were enabled to gather that Mr Waddell had carried a position with his new sword which had proved impregnable to civilian assault.

Only Bobby Little was silent. In all this genial symposium there had been no word of the spur which was inciting him — and doubtless the others — along the present weary and monotonous path; and on the whole he was glad that it should be so. None of us care to talk, even privately, about the Dream of Honour and the Hope of Glory. The only difference between Bobby and the others was that while they could cover up their aspirations with a jest, Bobby must say all that was in his heart, or keep silent. So he held his peace.

A tall figure loomed against the starlit sky, and Captain Wagstaffe, who had been out in the trench, spoke quickly to Major Kemp —

"I think we had better get to our places, sir. Some criminal has cut my alarm-cord!"

*   *   *   *

Five minutes previously, Private Bain, lulled to a sense of false security by the stillness of the night, had opened his eyes, which had been closed for purposes of philosophic reflection, to find himself surrounded by four ghostly figures in greatcoats. With creditable presence of mind he jerked his alarm-cord. But, alas! the cord came with his hand.

He was now a prisoner, and his place in the scout-line was being used as a point of deployment for the attacking force.

"We're extended right along the line now," said Captain Mackintosh to Simson. "I can't wait any longer for Shand: he has probably lost himself. The sentries are all behind us. Pass the word along to crawl forward. Every man to keep as low as he can, and dress by the right. No one to charge unless he hears my whistle, or is fired on."

The whispered word — Captain Mackintosh knows when to whisper quite as well as Captain Shand — runs down the line, and presently we begin to creep forward, stooping low. Sometimes we halt; sometimes we swing back a little; but on the whole we progress. Once there is a sudden exclamation. A highly-strung youth, crouching in a field drain, has laid his hand upon what looks and feels like a clammy human face, lying recumbent and staring heavenward. Too late, he recognises a derelict scarecrow with a turnip head. Again, there is a pause while the extreme right of the line negotiates an unexpected barbed-wire fence. Still, we move on, with enormous caution. We are not certain where the trenches are, but they must be near. At any moment a crackling volley may leap out upon us. Pulses begin to beat.

In the trench itself eyes are strained and ears cocked. It is an eerie sensation to know that men are near you, and creeping nearer, yet remain inaudible and invisible. It is a very dark night. The moon appears to have gone to bed for good, and the stars are mostly covered. Men unconsciously endeavour to fan the darkness away with their hands, like mist. The broken ground in front, with the black woods beyond, might be concealing an army corps for all the watchers in the trenches can tell. Far away to the south a bright finger of light occasionally stabs the murky heavens. It is the searchlight of a British cruiser, keeping ceaseless vigil in the English Channel, fifteen miles away. If she were not there we should not be making-believe here with such comfortable deliberation. It would be the real thing.

Bobby Little, who by this time can almost discern

spiked German helmets in the gloom, stands tingling. On either side of him are ranged the men of his platoon — some eager, some sleepy, but all silent. For the first time he notices that in the distant woods ahead of him there is a small break — a mere gap — through which one or two stars are twinkling. If only he could contrive to get a line of sight direct to that patch of sky —

He moves a few yards along the trench, and brings his eye to the ground-level. No good: a bush intervenes, fifteen yards away. He moves further and tries again.

Suddenly, for a brief moment, against the dimly illuminated scrap of horizon, he descries a human form, clad in a kilt, advancing stealthily. . . .

Number one Platoon — at the enemy in front — rapid fire!"

He is just in time. There comes an over-wrought roar of musketry all down the line of trenches. Simultaneously, a solid wall of men rises out of the earth not fifty yards away, and makes for the trenches with a long-drawn battle yell.

Make-believe has its thrills as well as the genuine article.

And so home to bed. McSnape duly became a lance-corporal, while Dunshie resigned his post as a scout and returned to duty with the company.

CHAPTER ELEVEN

OLYMPUS

UNDER THIS DESIGNATION it is convenient to lump the whole heavenly host which at present orders our goings and shapes our ends. It includes —
(1) The War Office;
(2) The Treasury;
(3) The Army Ordnance Office;
(4) Our Divisional Office;
— and other more local and immediate homes of mystery.

The Olympus which controls the destinies of "K(1)" differs in many respects from the Olympus of antiquity, but its celestial inhabitants appear to have at least two points in common with the original body — namely, a childish delight in upsetting one another's arrangements, and an untimely sense of humour when dealing with mortals.

So far as our researches have gone, we have been able to classify Olympus, roughly, into three departments —

(1) Round Game Department (including Dockets, Indents, and all official correspondence).
(2) Fairy Godmother Department.
(3) Practical Joke Department.

The outstanding feature of the Round Game Department is its craving for irrelevant information and its passion for detail. "Open your hearts to us," say the officials of the Department; "unburden your souls; keep nothing from us — and you will find us most accommodating. But stand on your dignity; decline to particularise; hold back one irrelevant detail — and it will go hard with you! Listen, and we will explain the rules of the game. Think of something you want immediately — say the command of a brigade, or a couple of washers for the lock of a machine-gun — and apply to us. The application must be made in writing, upon the Army Form provided for the purpose, and in triplicate. *And* — you must put in all the details you can possibly think of."

For instance, in the case of the machine-gun washers — by the way, in applying for them, you must call them *Gun, Machine, Light Vickers, Washers for lock of, two*. That is the way we always talk at the Ordnance Office. An Ordnance officer refers to his wife's mother as *Law, Mother-in-, one* — you should state when the old washers were lost, and by whom; also why they were lost, and where they are now. Then write a short history of the machine-gun from which they were lost, giving date and place of birth, together with a statement of the exact number of rounds which it has fired — a machine-gun fires about five hundred rounds a minute — adding the name and military record of the pack-animal which usually carries it. When you have filled up this document you forward it to the proper quarter and await results.

The game then proceeds on simple and automatic lines. If your application is referred back to you not more that five times, and if you get your washers within three months of the date of application, you are the winner. If you get something else instead — say an aeroplane, or a hundred wash-hand basins — it is a draw. But the chances are that you lose.

Consider. By the rules of the game, if Olympus can

think of a single detail which has not been thought of by you — for instance, if you omit to mention that the lost washers were circular in shape and had holes through the middle — you are *ipso facto* disqualified, under Rule One. Rule Two, also, is liable to trip you up. Possibly you may have written the pack-mule's name in small block capitals, instead of ordinary italics underlined in red ink, or put the date in Roman figures instead of Arabic numerals. If you do this, your application is referred back to you, and you lose a life. And even if you survive Rules One and Two, Rule Three will probably get you in the end. Under its provision your application must be framed in such language and addressed in such a manner that it passes through every department and sub-department of Olympus before it reaches the right one. The rule has its origin in the principle which governs the passing of wine at well-regulated British dinner-tables. That is, if you wish to offer a glass of port to your neighbour on your right, you hand the decanter to the neighbour on your left, so that the original object of your hospitality receives it, probably empty, only after a complete circuit of the table. In the present instance, the gentleman upon your right is the President of the Washer Department, situated somewhere in the Army Ordnance Office, the remaining guests representing the other centres of Olympian activity. For every department your application misses, you lose a life, three lost lives amounting to disqualification.

When the washers are issued, however, the port-wine rule is abandoned; and the washers are despatched to you, in defiance of all the laws of superstition and tradition, "widdershins", or counter-clockwise. No wonder articles thus jeopardised often fail to reach their destination!

Your last fence comes when you receive a document from Olympus announcing that your washers are now prepared for you, and that if you will sign and return the enclosed receipt they will be sent off upon their last journey. You are now in the worst dilemma of all. Olympus will not disgorge your washers until it has your receipt. On the other hand, if you send the receipt, Olympus can always win the game by losing the washers, and saying that *you* have got them. In the face of your own receipt you cannot very well deny this. So you lose your washers, and the game, and are also made liable for the misappropriation of two washers, for which Olympus holds your receipt.

Truly, the gods play with loaded dice.

On the whole, the simplest (and almost universal) plan is to convey a couple of washers from someone else's gun.

The game just described is played chiefly by officers; but this is a democratic age, and the rank and file are now occasionally permitted to take part.

For example, boots. Private McSplae is the possessor, we will say, of a pair of flat feet, or arched insteps, or other military incommodities, and his regulation boots do not fit him. More than that, they hurt him exceedingly, and as he is compelled to wear them through daily marches of several miles, they gradually wear a hole in his heel, or a groove in his instep, or a gathering on his great toe. So he makes the first move in the game, and reports sick — "sair feet".

The Medical Officer, a terribly efficient individual, keenly — sometimes too keenly — alert for signs of malingering, takes a cursory glance at McSplae's feet, and directs the patient's attention to the healing properties of soap and water. McSplae departs, grumbling, and re-appears on sick parade a few days later, palpably worse. This time, the M.O. being a little less pressed with work, McSplae is given a dressing for his feet, coupled with a recommendation to procure a new pair of boots without delay. If McSplae is a novice in regimental diplomacy, he will thereupon address himself to his platoon sergeant, who will consign him, eloquently, to a destination where only boots with asbestos soles will be of any use. If he is an old hand, he will simply cut his next parade, and will thus, rather ingeniously, obtain access to his company commander, being brought up before him at orderly-room next morning as a defaulter. To his captain he explains, with simple dignity, that he absented himself from parade because he found himself unable to "rise up" from his bed. He then endeavours, by hurriedly unlacing his boots, to produce his feet as evidence; but is frustrated, and awarded three extra fatigues for not formally reporting himself sick to the orderly sergeant. The real point at issue, namely, the unsuitability of McSplae's boots, again escapes attention.

There the matter rests until, a few days later, McSplae falls out on a long regimental route-march, and hobbles home, chaperoned by a not ungrateful lance-corporal, in a state of semi-collapse. This time the M.O. reports to the captain that Private McSplae will be unfit for further duty until he is provided with a proper pair of boots. Are there no boots in the quartermaster's store?

The captain explains that there are plenty of boots, but that under the rules of the present round game no one has any power to issue them. (This rule was put in to prevent the game from becoming too easy, like the spot-barred rule in billiards.) It is a fact well known to Olympus that no regimental officer can be trusted with boots. Not even the colonel can gain access to the regimental boot store. For all Olympus can tell, he might draw a pair of boots and wear them himself, or dress his children up in them, or bribe the brigadier with them, instead of issuing them to Private McSplae. No, Olympus thinks it wiser not to put temptation in the way of underpaid officers. So the boots remain locked up, and the taxpayer is protected.

But to be just, there is always a solution to an Olympian enigma, if you have the patience to go on looking for it. In this case the proper proceeding is for all concerned, including the prostrate McSplae, to wait patiently for a Board to sit. No date is assigned for this event, but it is bound to occur sooner or later, like a railway accident or an eclipse of the moon. So one day, out of a cloudless sky, a Board materialises, and sits on McSplae's boots. If McSplae's company commander happens to be president of the Board the boots are condemned, and the portals of the quartermaster's store swing open for a brief moment to emit a new pair.

When McSplae comes out of hospital, the boots, provided no one has appropriated them during the term of his indisposition, are his. He puts them on, to find that they pinch him in the same place as the old pair.

Then there is the Fairy Godmother Department, which supplies us with unexpected treats. It is the smallest department on Olympus, and, like most philanthropic institutions, is rather unaccountable in the manner in which it distributes its favours. It is somewhat hampered in its efforts, too, by the Practical Joke Department, which appears to exercise a sort of general right of interference all over Olympus. For instance, the Fairy Godmother Department decrees that officers from Indian regiments, who were home on leave when the War broke out and were commandeered for service with the Expeditionary Force, shall continue to draw pay on the Indian scale, which is considerably higher than that which prevails at home. So far, so good. But the Practical Joke Department hears of this, and scents an opportunity, in the form of "deductions". It promptly bleeds the beneficiaire of certain sums per day, for quarters, horse allowance, forage, and the like. It is credibly reported that one of these warriors, on emerging from a week's purgatory in a Belgian trench, found that his accommodation therein had been charged against him, under the head of "lodgings", at the rate of two shillings and threepence a night!

But sometimes the Fairy Godmother Department gets a free hand. Like a benevolent maiden aunt, she unexpectedly drops a twenty-pound note into your account at Cox's Bank, murmuring something vague about "additional outfit allowance"; and as Mr Cox makes a point of backing her up in her little secret, you receive a delightful surprise next time you open your pass-book.

She has the family instinct for detail, too, this Fairy Godmother. Perhaps the electric light in your bedroom fails, and for three days you have to sit in the dark or purchase candles. An invisible but observant little cherub notes this fact; and long afterwards a postal order for tenpence flutters down upon you from Olympus, marked "light allowance". Once Bobby Little received a mysterious postal order for one-and-fivepence. It was in the early days of his novitiate, before he had ceased to question the workings of Providence. So he made inquiries, and after prolonged investigation discovered the source of the windfall. On field service an officer is entitled to a certain sum per day as "field allowance". In barracks, however, possessing a bedroom and other indoor comforts, he receives no such gratuity. Now Bobby had once been compelled to share his room for a few nights with a newly-joined and homeless subaltern. He was thus temporarily rendered the owner of only half a bedroom. Or, to put it another way, only half of him was able to sleep in barracks. Obviously, then, the other half was on field service, and Bobby was therefore entitled to half field allowance. Hence the one-and-fivepence. I tell you, little escapes them on Olympus. So does much, but that is another story.

Last of all comes the Practical Joke Department. It covers practically all of one side of Olympus — the shady side.

The jokes usually take the form of an order, followed by a counter-order. For example —

In his magisterial days Ayling, of whom we have previously heard, was detailed by his Headmaster to undertake the organisation of a school corps to serve as a unit of the Officers' Training Corps — then one of the spoilt bantlings of the War Office. Being a vigorous and efficient young man, Ayling devoted four weeks of his summer holiday to a course of training with a battalion of regulars at Aldershot. During that period, as the prospective commander of a company, he was granted the pay and provisional rank of captain, which all will admit was handsome enough treatment. Three months later, when after superhuman struggles he had pounded his youthful legionaries into something like efficiency, his appointment to a commission was duly confirmed, and he found himself gazetted — Second Lieutenant. In addition to this, he was required to refund to the Practical Joke Department the difference between second lieutenant's pay and the captain's pay which he had received during his month's training at Aldershot!

But in these strenuous days the Department has no time for baiting individuals. It has two or three millions of men to sharpen its wit upon. Its favourite pastime at present is a sort of giant's game of chess, the fair face of England serving as board, and the various units of the K. armies as pieces. The object of the players is to get each piece through as many squares as possible in a given time, it being clearly understood that no move shall count unless another piece is evicted in the process. For instance, we, the xth Brigade of the yth Division, are suddenly uprooted from Billets at A and planted down in barracks at B, displacing the pth Brigade of the qth Division in the operation. We have barely cleaned up after the pth — an Augean task — and officers have just concluded messing, furnishing, and laundry arrangements with the local *banditti,* when the Practical Joke Department, with its tongue in its cheek, bids us prepare to go under canvas at C. Married officers hurriedly despatch advance parties, composed of their wives, to secure houses or lodgings in the bleak and inhospitable environs of their new station; while a rapidly ageing Mess President concludes yet another demoralising bargain with a ruthless and omnipotent caterer. Then — this is the cream of the joke — the day before we expect to move, the Practical Joke Department puts out a playful hand and sweeps us all into some half-completed huts at D, somewhere at the other end of the Ordnance map, and leaves us there, with a happy chuckle, to sink or swim in an Atlantic of mud.

So far as one is able to follow the scoring of the game, some of the squares in the chess-board are of higher value than others. For instance, if you are dumped down into comparatively modern barracks at Aldershot, which, although they contain no furniture, are at least weatherproof and within reach of shops, the Practical Joke Department scores one point. Barracks condemned as unsafe and insanitary before the war, but now reckoned highly eligible, count three points; rat-ridden billets count five. But if you can manoeuvre your helpless pawns into Mudsplosh Camp, you receive ten whole points, with a bonus of two points thrown in if you can effect the move without previous notice of any kind.

We are in Mudsplosh Camp today. In transferring us here the Department secured full points, including bonus.

Let it not be supposed, however, that we are decrying our present quarters. Mudsplosh Camp is — or is going to be — a nobly planned and admirably equipped military centre. At present it consists of some three hundred wooden huts, in all stages of construction, covering about twenty acres of high moorland. The huts are heated with stoves, and will be delightfully warm when we get some coal. They are lit by — or rather wired for — electric light. Meanwhile a candle-end does well enough for a room only a hundred feet long. There are numerous other adjuncts to our comfort — wash-houses, for instance. These will be invaluable, when the water is laid on. For the present, there is a capital standpipe not a hundred yards away; and all you have do, if you want an invigorating scrub, is to wait your turn for one of the two tin basins supplied to each fifty men, and then splash to your heart's content. There is a spacious dining-hall; and as soon as the roof is on, our successors, or their successors, will make merry therein. Meanwhile, there are worse places to eat one's dinner than the floor — the mud outside, for instance.

The stables are lofty and well ventilated. At least we are sure they will be. Pending their completion the horses and mules are very comfortable, picketed on the edge of the moor. . . . After all, there are only sixty of them; and most of them have rugs; and it can't possibly go on snowing for ever.

The only other architectural feature of the camp is the steriliser, which has been working night and day ever since we arrived. No, it does not sterilise water or milk, or anything of that kind — only blankets. Those men standing in a *queue* at its door are carrying their bedding. (Yes, quite so. When blankets are passed from regiment to regiment for months on end, in a camp where opportunities for ablution are not lavish, these little things will happen.)

You put the blankets in at one end of the steriliser, turn the necessary handles, and wait. In due course the blankets emerge, steamed, dried and thoroughly purged. At least, that is the idea. But listen to Privates Ogg and Hogg, in one of their celebrated cross-talk duologues.

Ogg (examining his blanket). "They're a' there yet. See!"

Hogg (an optimist). "Aye but they must have gotten an awfu' fricht!"

But then people like Ogg are never satisfied with anything.

However, *the* feature of this camp is the mud. That is why it counts ten points. There was no mud, of course, before the camp was constructed — only dry turf, and wild yellow gorse, and fragrant heather. But the Pratical Joke Department were not to be discouraged by the superficial beauties of nature. They knew that if you crowd a large number of human dwellings close together, and refrain from constructing any roads or drains as a preliminary, and fill these buildings with troops in the rainy season, you will soon have as much mud as ever you require. And they were quite right. The depth varies from a few inches to about a foot. On the outskirts of the camp, however, especially by the horse lines or going through a gate, you may find yourself up to your knees. But, after all, what is mud? Most of the officers have gumboots, and the men will probably get used to it. Life in K(1) is largely composed of getting used to things.

In the more exclusive and fashionable districts — round about the Orderly-room, and the Canteen, and the Guard-room — elevated "duck-walks" are laid down, along which we delicately pick our way. It would warm the heart of a democrat to observe the ready — nay, hasty — courtesy with which an officer, on meeting a private carrying two overflowing buckets of kitchen refuse, steps down into the mud to let his humble brother-in-arms pass. Where there are no duck-walks, we employ planks laid across the mud. In comparatively dry weather these planks lie some two or three inches below the mud, and much innocent amusement may be derived from trying to locate them. In wet weather, however, the planks float to the surface, and then of course everything is plain sailing. When it snows, we feel for the planks with our feet. If we find them we perform an involuntary and unpremeditated ski-ing act: if we fail, we wade to our quarters through a sort of neapolitan ice — snow on top, mud underneath.

Our parade-ground is a mud-flat in front of the huts. Here we take our stand each morning, sinking steadily deeper until the order is given to move off. Then the battalion extricates itself with one tremendous squelch, and we proceed to the labours of the day.

Seriously, though — supposing the commanding officer were to be delayed one morning at orderly-room, and were to ride on to the parade-ground twenty minutes late, what would he find? Nothing! Nothing but a great *parterre* of glengarries, perched upon the mud in long parallel rows, each glengarry flanked on the left-hand side by the muzzle of a rifle at the slope. (That detached patch over there on the left front, surrounded by air bubbles, is the band. That cavity like the crater of an extinct volcano, in Number One platoon of A Company, was once Private Mucklewame.)

Any yet people talk about the sinking of the *Birkenhead!*

This morning someone in the Department has scored another ten points. Word has just been received that we are to move again tomorrow — to a precisely similar set of huts about a hundred yards away!

They are mad wags on Olympus.

CHAPTER TWELVE

. . . AND SOME FELL
BY THE WAYSIDE

"*FIRING PARRTY, revairse arrms!*"

Thus the platoon sergeant — a little anxiously; for we are new to this feat, and only rehearsed it for a few minutes this morning.

It is a sunny afternoon in late February. The winter of our discontent is past. (At least, we hope so.) Comfortless months of training are safely behind us, and lo! we have grown from a fortuitous concourse of atoms to a cohesive unit of fighting men. Spring is coming; our blood runs quicker; active service is within measurable distance; and the future beckons to us with both hands to step down at last into the arena, and try our fortune amid the uncertain but illimitable chances of the greatest game in the world.

To all of us, that is, save one.

The road running up the hill from the little mortuary is lined on either side by members of our company, specklessly turned out and standing to attention. At the foot of the slope a gun-carriage is waiting, drawn by two great dray horses and controlled by a private of the Royal Artillery, who looks incongruously perky and cockney amid that silent, kilted assemblage. The firing party form a short lane from the gun-carriage to the door of the mortuary. In response to the sergeant's command, each man turns over his rifle, and setting

114

the muzzle carefully upon his right boot — after all, it argues no extra respect to the dead to get your barrel filled with mud — rests his hands upon the butt-plate and bows his head, as laid down in the King's Regulations.

The bearers move slowly down the path from the mortuary, and place the coffin upon the gun-carriage. Upon the lid lie a very dingy glengarry, a stained leather belt, and a bayonet. They are humble trophies, but we pay them as much reverence as we would to the *bâton* and cocked hat of a field-marshal, for they are the insignia of a man who has given his life for his country.

On the hill-top above us, where the great military hospital rears its clock-tower four-square to the sky, a line of convalescents, in natty blue uniforms with white facings and red ties, lean over the railings deeply interested. Some of them are bandaged, others are in slings, and all are more or less maimed. They follow the obsequies below with critical approval. They have been present at enough hurried and promiscuous interments of late — more than one of them has only just escaped being the central figure at one of these functions — that they are capable of appreciating a properly conducted funeral at its true value.

"They're putting away a bloomin' Jock," remarks a gentleman with an empty sleeve.

"And very nice, too!" responds another on crutches, as the firing party present arms with creditable precision. "Not 'arf a bad bit of eye-wash at all for a bandy-legged lot of coal-shovellers."

"That lot's out of K (1)," explains a well-informed invalid with his head in bandages. "Pretty 'ot stuff they're gettin'. *Très moutarde!* Now we're off."

The signal is passed up the road to the band, who are waiting at the head of the procession, and the pipes break into a lament. Corporals step forward and lay four wreaths upon the coffin — one from each company. Not a man in the battalion has failed to contribute his penny to those wreaths; and pennies are not too common with us, especially on a Thursday, which comes just before pay-day. The British private is commonly reputed to spend all, or most of, his pocket-money upon beer. But I can tell you this, that if you give him his choice between buying himself a pint of beer and subscribing to a wreath, he will most decidedly go thirsty.

The serio-comic charioteer gives his reins a twitch, the horses wake up, and the gun-carriage begins to move slowly along the lane of mourners. As the dead private passes on his way the walls of the lane melt, and his comrades fall into their usual fours behind the gun-carriage.

So we pass up the hill towards the military cemetery, with the pipes wailing their hearts out, and the muffled drums marking the time of our regulation slow step. Each foot seems to hang in the air before the drums bid us put it down.

In the very rear of the procession you may see the company commander and three subalterns. They give no orders, and exact no attention. To employ a colloquialism, this is not their funeral.

Just behind the gun-carriage stalks a solitary figure in civilian clothes — the unmistakable "blacks" of an Elder of the Kirk. At first sight, you have a feeling that someone has strayed into the procession who has no right there. But no one has a better. The sturdy old man behind the coffin is named Adam Carmichael, and he is here, having travelled south from Dumbarton by the night train, to attend the funeral of his only son.

*   *   *   *

Peter Carmichael was one of the first to enlist in the regiment. There was another Carmichael in the same company, so Peter at roll-call was usually addressed by the sergeant as "Twenty-seven fufty-fower Carmichael", 2754 being his regimental number. The army does not encourage Christian names. When his attestation paper was filled up, he gave his age as nineteen; his address, vaguely, as Renfrewshire; and his trade, not without an air, as a "holder-on". To the mystified Bobby Little he entered upon a lengthy explanation of the term in a language composed entirely of vowels, from which that officer gathered, dimly, that holding-on had something to do with shipbuilding.

Upon the barrack square his platoon commander's attention was again drawn to Peter, owing to the passionate enthusiasm with which he performed the simplest evolutions, such as forming fours and sloping arms — military exercises which do not intrigue the average private to any great extent. Unfortunately, desire frequently outran performance. Peter was undersized, unmuscular, and extraordinarily clumsy. For a long time Bobby Little thought that Peter, like one or two of his comrades, was left-handed, so made allowances. Ultimately he discovered that his indulgence was misplaced: Peter was equally incompetent with either hand. He took longer in learning to fix bayonets or present arms than any other man in the platoon. To be fair, Nature had done little to help him. He was thirty-three inches round the chest, five feet four in height, and weighed possibly nine stone. His complexion was pasty, and, as Captain Wagstaffe remarked, you could hang your hat on any bone in his body. His eyesight was not all that the Regulations require, and on the musketry-range he was "put back", to his deep distress, "for further instruction". Altogether, if you had not known the doctor who passed him, you would have said it was a mystery how he passed the doctor.

But he possessed the one essential attribute of the

soldier. He had a big heart. He was keen. He allowed nothing to come between him and his beloved duties. ("He was aye daft for to go sojerin',") his father explained to Captain Blaikie; "but his mother would never let him away. He was ower wee, and ower young.") His rifle, buttons, and boots were always without blemish. Further, he was of the opinion that a merry heart goes all the way. He never sulked when the platoon were kept on parade five minutes after the breakfast bugle had sounded. He made no bones about obeying orders and saluting officers — acts of abasement which grated sorely at times upon his colleagues, who reverenced no one except themselves and their Union. He appeared to revel in muddy route-marches, and invariably provoked and led the choruses. The men called him "Wee Pe'er", and ultimately adopted him as a sort of company mascot. Whereat Pe'er's heart glowed; for when your associates attach a diminutive to your Christian name, you possess something which millionaires would gladly give half their fortunes to purchase.

And certainly he required all the social success he could win, for professionally Peter found life a rigorous affair. Sometimes, as he staggered into barracks after a long day, carrying a rifle made of lead and wearing a pair of boots weighing a hundredweight apiece, he dropped dead asleep on his bedding before he could eat his dinner. But he always hotly denied the imputation that he was "sick".

Time passed. The regiment was shaking down. Seven of Peter's particular cronies were raised to the rank of lance-corporal — but not Peter. He was "off the square" now — that is to say, he was done with recruit drill for ever. He possessed a sound knowledge of advance-guard and outpost work; his conduct-sheet was a blank page. But he was not promoted. He was "ower wee for a stripe", he told himself. For the present he must expect to be passed over. His chance would come later, when he had filled out a little and got rid of his cough.

The winter dragged on: the weather was appalling: the grousers gave tongue with no uncertain voice, each streaming field-day. But Wee Pe'er enjoyed it all. He did not care if it snowed ink. He was a "sojer".

One day, to his great delight, he was "warned for guard" — a particularly unpopular branch of a soldier's duties, for it means sitting in the guard-room for twenty-four hours at a stretch, fully dressed and accoutred, with intervals of sentry-go, usually in heavy rain, by way of exercise. When Peter's turn for sentry-go came on he splashed up and down his muddy beat — the battalion was in billets now, and the usual sentry's verandah was lacking — as proud as a peacock, saluting officers according to their rank, challenging stray civilians with great severity, and turning out the guard on the slightest provocation. He was at his post, soaked right through his greatcoat, when the orderly officer made his night round. Peter summoned his colleagues; the usual inspection of the guard took place; and the sleepy men were then dismissed to their fireside. Peter remained; the officer hesitated. He was supposed to examine the sentry in his knowledge of his duties. It was a profitless task as a rule. The tongue-tied youth merely gaped like a stranded fish, until the sergeant mercifully intervened, in some such words as these —

"This man, sirr, is liable to get over-excited when addressed by an officer."

Then, soothingly —

"Now, Jimmy, tell the officer what would ye dae in case of fire?"

"Present airrms!" announces the desperate James. Or else, almost tearfully, "I canna mind. I had it all fine just noo, but it's awa' oot o' ma heid!"

Therefore it was with no great sense of anticipation that the orderly officer said to Private Carmichael —

119

"Now, sentry, can you repeat any of your duties?"

Peter saluted, took a full breath, closed both eyes, and replied rapidly —

"For tae tak' chairge of all Government property within sicht of this guairdhoose tae turrn out the guaird for all arrmed pairties approaching also the commanding officer once a day tae salute all officers tae challenge all pairsons approaching this post tae —"

His recital was interrupted by a fit of coughing.

"Thank you," said the officer hastily; "that will do. Good night!"

Peter, not sure whether it would be correct to say "good night" too, saluted again, and returned to his cough.

"I say," said the officer, turning back, "you have a shocking cold."

"Och, never heed it, sirr," gasped Peter politely.

"Call the sergeant," said the officer.

The fat sergeant came out of the guard-house again, buttoning his tunic.

"Sirr?"

"Take this man off sentry-duty and roast him at the guard-room fire."

"I will, sirr," replied the sergeant; and added paternally —

"This man has no right for to be here at all. He should have reported sick when warned for guard; but he would not. He is very attentive to his duties, sirr."

"Good boy!" said the officer to Peter. "I wish we had more like you."

Wee Pe'er blushed, his teeth momentarily ceased chattering, his heart swelled. Appearances to the contrary, he felt warm all through. The sergeant laid a fatherly hand upon his shoulder.

"Go you your ways intil the guard-room, boy," he commanded, "and send oot Dunshie. He'll no hurt. Get close in ahint the stove, or you'll be for Cambridge!"

(The last phrase carries no academic significance. It simply means that you are likely to become an inmate of the great Cambridge Hospital at Aldershot.)

Peter, feeling thoroughly disgraced, cast an appealing look at the officer.

"In you go!" said that martinet.

Peter silently obeyed. It was the only time in his life that he ever felt mutinous.

A month later Brigade Training set in with customary severity. The life of company officers became a burden. They spent hours in thick woods with their followers, taking cover, ostensibly from the enemy, in reality from brigade-majors and staff officers. A subaltern never tied his platoon in a knot but a general came trotting round the corner. The wet weather had ceased, and a biting east wind reigned in its stead.

On one occasion an elaborate night operation was arranged. Four battalions were to assemble at a given point five miles from camp, and then advance in column across country by the light of the stars to a position indicated on the map, where they were to deploy and dig themselves in! It sounded simple enough in operation orders; but when you try to move four thousand troops — even well-trained troops — across three miles of broken country on a pitch-dark night, there is always a possibility that someone will get mislaid. On this particular occasion a whole battalion lost itself without any delay or difficulty whatsoever. The other three were compelled to wait for two hours and a half, stamping their feet and blowing on their fingers, while overheated staff officers scoured the country for truants. They were discovered at last waiting virtuously at the wrong rendezvous, three-quarters of a mile away. The brazen-hatted strategist who drew up the operation orders had given the point of assembly for the brigade as: ... *the field* S.W. *of* WELLINGTON

WOOD *and due* E. *of* HANGMAN'S COPSE, *immediately below the first* O *in* GHOSTLY BOTTOM, — but omitted to underline the O indicated. The result was that three battalion commanders assembled at the O in "ghostly", while the fourth, ignoring the adjective in favour of the noun, took up his station at the first O in "bottom".

The operations had been somewhat optimistically timed to end at 11 p.m., but by the time that the four battalions had effected a most unlovely tryst, it was close on ten, and beginning to rain. The consequence was that the men got home to bed, soaked to the skin, and asking the Powers Above rhetorical questions, at three o'clock in the morning.

Next day Brigade Orders announced that the movement would be continued at nightfall, by the occupation of the hastily-dug trenches, followed by a night attack upon the hill in front. The captured position would then be retrenched.

When the tidings went round, fourteen of the more quick-witted spirits of A Company hurriedly paraded before the Medical Officer and announced that they were "sick in the stomach." Seven more discovered abrasions upon their feet, and proffered their sores for inspection, after the manner of Oriental mendicants. One skrimshanker, despairing of producing any bodily ailment, rather ingeniously assaulted a comrade-in-arms, and was led away, deeply grateful, to the guard-room. Wee Peter, who in the course of last night's operations had stumbled into an old trench half-filled with ice-cold water, and whose temperature today, had he known it, was a hundred and two, paraded with his company at the appointed time. The company, he reflected, would get a bad name if too many men reported sick at once.

Next day he was absent from parade. He was "for Cambridge" at last.

Before he died, he sent for the officer who had

befriended him, and supplemented, or rather corrected, some of the information contained in his attestation paper.

He lived in Dumbarton, not Renfrewshire. He was just sixteen. He was not — this confession cost him a great effort — a full-blown "holder-on" at all; only an apprentice. His father was "weel kent" in the town of Dumbarton, being a chief engineer, employed by a great firm of shipbuilders to extend new machinery on trial trips.

Needless to say, he made a great fight. But though his heart was big enough, his body was too frail. As they say on the sea, he was over-engined for his beam.

And so, three days later, the simple soul of Twenty-seven fifty-four Carmichael, A Company, was transferred, on promotion, to another company — the great Company of Happy Warriors who walk the Elysian Fields.

*   *   *   *

"Firing parrty, one round blank — load!"

There is a rattle of bolts, and a dozen barrels are pointed heavenwards. The company stands rigid, except the buglers, who are beginning to finger their instruments.

"Fire!"

There is a crackling volley, and the pipes break into a brief, sobbing wail. Wayfarers upon the road below look up curiously. One or two young females with perambulators come hurrying across the grass, exhorting apathetic babies to sit up and admire the pretty funeral.

Twice more the rifles ring out. The pipes cease their wailing, and there is an expectant silence.

The drum-major crooks his little finger, and eight

bugles come to the "ready." Then "Last Post", the requiem of every soldier of the King, swells out, sweet and true.

The echoes lose themselves among the dripping pines. The chaplain closes his book, takes off his spectacles, and departs.

Old Carmichael permits himself one brief look into his son's grave, resumes his crape-bound tall hat, and turns heavily away. He finds Captain Blaikie's hand waiting for him. He grips it, and says —

"Weel, the laddie has had a grand sojer's funeral. His mother will be pleased to hear that."

He passes on, and shakes hands with the platoon sergeant and one or two of Peter's cronies. He declines an invitation to the Sergeants' Mess.

"I hae a trial-trup the morn," he explains. "I must be steppin'. God keep ye all, brave lads!"

The old gentleman sets off down the station road. The company falls in, and we march back to barracks, leaving Wee Pe'er — the first name on our Roll of Honour — alone in his glory beneath the Hampshire pines.

CHAPTER THIRTEEN

CONCERT PITCH

WE HAVE ONLY two topics of conversation now — the date of our departure, and our destination. Both are wrapped in mystery so profound that our range of speculation is practically unlimited.

Conjecture rages most fiercely in the Officers' Mess, which is in touch with sources of unreliable information not accessible to the rank and file. The humblest subaltern appears to be possessed of a friend at court, or a cousin in the Foreign Office, or an aunt in the Intelligence Department, from whom he can derive fresh and entirely different information each weekend leave.

Master Cockerell, for instance, has it straight from the Horse Guards that we are going out next week — as a single unit, to be brigaded with two seasoned regiments in Flanders. He has a considerable following.

Then comes Waddell, who has been informed by the Assistant sub-Editor of an evening journal widely read in his native Dundee, that The First Hundred Thousand are to sit here, eating the bread of impatience, until The First Half Million are ready. Thereupon we shall break through our foeman's line at a point hitherto unassailed and known only to the scribe of Dundee, and proceed to roll up the German Empire as if it were a carpet, into some obscure corner of the continent of Europe.

Bobby Little, not the least of whose gifts is a soaring imagination, has mapped out a sort of strategical Cook's Tour for us, beginning with the sack of Constantinople, and ending, after a glorified route-march up the Danube and down the Rhine, which shall include a pitched battle once a week and a successful siege once a month, with a "circus" entry into Potsdam.

Captain Wagstaffe offers no opinion, but darkly recommends us to order pith helmets. However, we are rather suspicious of Captain Wagstaffe these days. He suffers from an over-developed sense of humour.

The rank and file keep closer to earth in their prognostications. In fact, some of them cleave to the dust. With them it is a case of hope deferred. Quite half of them enlisted under the firm belief that they would forthwith be furnished with a rifle and ammunition and despatched to a vague place called "the front", there to take pot-shots at the Kaiser. That was in early August. It is now early April, and they are still here, performing monotonous evolutions and chafing under the bonds of discipline. Small wonder that they have begun to doubt, these simple souls, if they are ever going out at all. Private McSlattery put the general opinion in a nutshell.

"This regiment," he announced, "is no' for the front at all. We're jist tae bide here, for tae be inspeckit by Chinese Ministers and other heathen bodies!"

This withering summary of the situation was evoked by the fact that we had once been called out, and kept on parade for two hours in a north-east wind, for the edification of a bevy of spectacled dignitaries from the Far East. For the Scottish artisan the word "minister", however, has only one significance; so it is probable that McSlattery's strictures were occasioned by sectarian, rather than racial, prejudice.

Still, whatever our ultimate destinaton and fate may be, the fact remains that we are now as fit for active service as seven months' relentless schooling, under make-believe conditions, can render us. We shall have to begin all over again, we know, when we find ourselves up against the real thing, but we have at least been thoroughly grounded in the rudiments of our profession. We can endure hail, rain, snow, and vapour; we can march and dig with the best; we have mastered the first principles of musketry; we can advance in an extended line without losing touch or bunching; and we have ceased to regard an order as an insult, or obedience as a degradation. We eat when we can and what we get, and we sleep whenever we happen to find ourselves lying. That is something. But there are certain military accomplishments which can only be taught us by the enemy. Taking cover, for instance. When the thin, intermittent crackle of blank ammunition shall have been replaced by the whistle of real bullets, we shall get over our predilection for sitting up and taking notice. The conversation of our neighbour, or the deplorable antics of B Company on the neighbouring skyline, will interest us not at all. We shall get down, and stay down.

We shall also be relieved of the necessity of respecting the property of those exalted persons who surround their estates with barbed wire, and put up notices, even now, warning off troops. At present we either crawl painfully through that wire, tearing our kilts and lacerating our legs, or go round another way. "Oot there", such unwholesome deference will be a thing of the past. Would that the wire-setters were going out with us. We would give them the place of honour in the forefront of battle!

We have fired a second musketry course, and are now undergoing Divisional Training, with the result that we take our walks abroad several thousands strong, greatly to the derangement of local traffic.

Considered all round, Divisional Training is the

pleasantest form of soldiering that we have yet encountered. We parade bright and early, at full battalion strength, accompanied by our scouts, signallers, machine-guns, and transport, and march off at the appointed minute to the starting-point. Here we slip into our place in an already moving column, with three thousand troops in front of us and another two thousand behind, and tramp to our point of deployment. We feel pleasantly thrilled. We are no longer a battalion out on a route-march: we are members of a White Army, or a Brown Army, hastening to frustrate the designs of a Blue Army, or a Pink Army, which has landed (according to the General Idea issued from Headquarters) at Portsmouth, and is reported to have slept at Great Snoreham, only ten miles away, last night.

Meanwhile our Headquarters Staff is engaged in the not always easy task of "getting into touch" with the enemy — *anglice*, finding him. It is extraordinary how elusive a force of several thousand troops can be, especially when you are picking your way across a defective half-inch map, and the commanders of the opposing forces cherish dissimilar views as to where the point of encounter is supposed to be. However, contact is at length established; and if it is not time to go home, we have a battle.

Various things may now happen to you. You may find yourself detailed for the Firing-line. In that case your battalion will take open order; and you will advance, principally upon your stomach, over hill and dale until you encounter the enemy, doing likewise. Both sides then proceed to discharge blank ammunition into one another's faces at a range, if possible, of about five yards, until the "cease-fire" sounds.

Or you may find yourself in Support. In that case you are held back until the battle has progressed a stage or two, when you advance with fixed bayonets to prod your own firing line into a further display of valour and agility.

Or you may be detailed as Reserve. Membership of Brigade Reserve should be avoided. You are liable to be called upon at any moment to forsake the sheltered wood or lee of a barn under which you are huddling, and double madly up a hill or along a side-road, tripping heavily over ingenious entanglements composed of the telephone wires of your own signallers, to enfilade some unwary detachment of the enemy or repel a flank attack. On the other hand, if you are ordered to act as Divisional Reserve, you may select the softest spot on the hillside behind which you are sheltering, get out your haversack ration, and prepare to spend an extremely peaceful (or extremely dull) day. Mimic warfare enjoys one enormous advantage over the genuine article: battles — provided you are not out for the night — *must always* end in time for the men to get back to their dinners at five o'clock. Under this inexorable law it follows that, by the time the General has got into touch with the enemy and brought his firing line, supports, and local reserves into action, it is time to go home. So about three o'clock the bugles sound, and the combatants, hot and grimy, fall back into close order at the point of deployment, where they are presently joined by the Divisional Reserve, blue-faced and watery-eyed with cold. This done, principals and understudies, casting envious glances at one another, form one long column of route and set out for home, in charge of the subalterns. The senior officers trot off to the "pow-wow", there, with the utmost humility and deference, to extol their own tactical dispositions, belittle the achievements of the enemy, and impugn the veracity of one another.

Thus the day's work ends. Our divisional column, with its trim, sturdy, infantry battalions, its jingling cavalry and artillery, its real live staff, and its imposing transport train, sets us thinking, by sheer force of contrast, of that dim and distant time seven months ago, when we wrestled perspiringly all through long and hot September days, on a dusty barrack square, with squad upon squad of dazed and refractory barbarians, who only ceased shuffling their feet in order to expectorate. And these are the self-same men! Never was there a more complete vindication of the policy of pegging away.

*   *   *   *

So much for the effect of its training upon the regiment as a whole. But when you come to individuals, certain of whom we have encountered and studied in this rambling narrative, you find it impossible to generalise. Your one unshakable conclusion is that it takes all sorts to make a type.

There are happy, careless souls like McLeary and Hogg. There are conscientious but slow-moving worthies like Mucklewame and Budge. There are drunken wasters like — well, we need name no names. We have got rid of most of these, thank heaven! There are simple-minded enthusiasts of the breed of Wee Pe'er, for whom the sheer joy of "sojering" still invests dull routine and hard work with a glamour of their own. There are the old hands, versed in every labour-saving (and duty-shirking) device. There are the feckless and muddle-headed, making heavy weather of the simplest tasks. There is another class, which divides its time between rising to the position of sergeant and being reduced to the ranks, for causes which need not be specified. There is yet another, which knows its drill-book backwards, and can grasp the details of a tactical scheme as quickly as a seasoned officer, but remains in the ruck because it has not sufficient force of character to handle so much as a sentry-group. There are men, again, with initiative but no endurance, and others with endurance but no initiative. Lastly, there are men, and a great many of them, who appear to be quite incapable of coherent thought, yet can handle machinery or any mechanical device to a marvel. Yes, we are a motley organisation.

But the great sifting and sorting machine into which we have been cast is shaking us all out into our appointed places. The efficient and authoritative rise to non-commissioned rank. The quick-witted and well-educated find employment on the Orderly Room staff, or among the scouts and signallers. The handy are absorbed into the transport, or become machine-gunners. The sedentary take posts as cooks or tailors, or officers' servants. The waster hews wood and draws water and empties swill-tubs. The great, mediocre, undistinguished majority merely go to stiffen the rank and file, and right nobly they do it. Each has its niche.

To take a few examples, we may begin with a typical member of the undistinguished majority. Such a one is that esteemed citizen of Wishaw, John Mucklewame. He is a rank-and-file man by training and instinct, but he forms a rare backbone for K(1). There are others, of more parts — Killick, for instance. Not long ago he was living softly, and driving a Rolls-Royce for a Duke. He is now a machine-gun sergeant, and a very good one. There is Dobie. He is a good mechanic, but short-legged and shorter-winded. He makes an excellent armourer.

Then there is Private Mellish. In his company roll he is described as "an actor". But his orbit in the theatrical firmament has never carried him outside his native Dunoon, where he follows the blameless but monotonous calling of a cinematograph operator. On enlistment he invited the attention of his platoon from the start by referring to his rear-rank man as "this young gentleman"; and despite all the dissuading influences of barrack-room society, his manners never fell below this standard. In a company where practically every man is addressed either as "Jock" or "Jimmy", he created a profound and lasting sensation one day by saying in a winning voice to Private Ogg —

"Do not stand on ceremony with me, Mr Ogg. Call me Cyril!"

For such an exotic there could only be one destination, and in due course Cyril became an officer's servant. He now polishes the buttons and washes the hose-tops of Captain Wagstaffe; and his elegant extracts amuse that student of human nature exceedingly.

Then comes a dour, silent, earnest specimen, whose name, incredible as it may appear, is McOstrich. He keeps himself to himself. He never smiles. He is not an old soldier, yet he performed like a veteran the very first day he appeared on parade. He carries out all orders with solemn thoroughness. He does not drink; he does not swear. His nearest approach to animation comes at church, where he sings the hymns — especially *O God, our help in ages past!* — as if he were author and composer combined. His harsh, rasping accent is certainly not that of a Highlander, nor does it smack altogether of the Clydeside. As a matter of fact he is not a Scotsman at all, though five out of six of us would put him down as such. Altogether he is a man of mystery; but the regiment could do with many more such.

Once, and only once, did he give us a peep behind the scenes. Private Burke of D Company, a cheery soul, who possesses the entirely Hibernian faculty of being able to combine a most fanatical and seditious brand of Nationalism with a genuine and ardent enthusiasm for the British Empire, one day made a contemptuous and ribald reference to the Ulster Volunteers and their leader. McOstrich, who was sitting on his bedding at the other side of the hut, promptly rose to his feet, crossed the floor in three strides, and silently felled the humorist to the earth. Plainly, if McOstrich comes safe through the war, he is prepared for another and grimmer campaign.

Lastly, that jack-of-all-trades and master of none, Private Dunshie. As already recorded, Dunshie's original calling had been that of a street news-vendor. Like all literary men, he was a Bohemian at heart. Routine wearied him; discipline galled him; the sight of work made him feel faint. After a month or two in the ranks he seized the first opportunity of escaping from the toils of his company, by volunteering for service as a Scout. A single experience of night operations in a dark wood, previously described, decided him to seek some milder employment. Observing that the regimental cooks appeared to be absolved, by virtue of their office, not only from all regimental parades, but from all obligations on the subject of correct attire and personal cleanliness, he volunteered for service in the kitchen. Here for a space — clad in shirt, trousers, and canvas shoes, unutterably greasy and waxing fat — he prospered exceedingly. But one sad day he was detected by the cook-sergeant, having just finished cleaning a flue, in the act of washing his hands in ten gallons of B Company's soup. Once more our versatile hero found himself turned adrift with brutal and agonising suddenness, and bidden to exercise his talents elsewhere.

After a fortnight's uneventful dreariness with his platoon, Dunshie joined the machine-gunners, because he had heard rumours that these were conveyed to and from their labours in limbered waggons. But he had been misinformed. It was the guns that were carried; the gunners invariably walked, sometimes carrying the guns and the appurtenances thereof. His very first day Dunshie was compelled to double across half a mile of boggy heathland carrying two large stones, meant to represent ammunition-boxes, from an imaginary waggon to a dummy gun. It is true that as soon as he was out of sight of the corporal he deposited the stones upon the ground, and ultimately proffered two others, picked up on nearing his destination, to the sergeant in charge of the proceedings; but even thus the work struck him as unreasonably exacting, and he resigned, by the simple process of cutting his next parade and being ignominiously returned to his company.

After an unsuccessful application for employment as a "buzzer", or signaller, Dunshie made trial of the regimental transport, where there was a shortage of drivers. He had strong hopes that in this way he would attain to permanent carriage exercise. But he was quickly undeceived. Instead of being offered a seat upon the box of a G.S. waggon, he was bidden to walk behind the same, applying the brake when necessary, for fourteen miles. The next day he spent cleaning stables, under a particularly officious corporal. On the third, he was instructed in the art of grooming a mule. On the fourth, he was left to perform this feat unaided, and the mule, acting under extreme provocation, kicked him in the stomach. On the fifth day he was returned to his company.

But Mecca was at hand. That very morning Dunshie's company commander received the following ukase from headquarters:

Officers commanding Companies will render to the Orderly Room without fail, by 9 A.M. tomorrow, the name of one man qualified to act as chiropodist to the Company.

Major Kemp scratched his nose in a dazed fashion, and looked over his spectacles at his Quartermaster-Sergeant.

"What in thunder will they ask for next?" he growled. "Have we got any tame chiropodists in the company, Rae?"

Quartermaster-Sergeant Rae turned over the Company roll.

"There is no — no — no man of that profession here, sirr," he reported, after scanning the document. "But," he added optimistically, "there is a machine-fitter and a glass-blower. Will I warn one of them?"

"I think we had better call for a volunteer first," said Major Kemp tactfully.

Accordingly, that afternoon upon parade, platoon commanders were bidden to hold a witch hunt, and smell out a chiropodist. But the enterprise terminated almost immediately; for Private Dunshie, caressing his injured abdomen in Number Three Platoon, heard the invitation, and quickly stepped forward.

"So you are a chiropodist as well as everything else, Dunshie!" said Ayling incredulously.

"That's right, sirr," assented Dunshie politely.

"Are you a professional?"

"No exactly that, sirr," was the modest reply.

"You just make a hobby of it?"

"Just that, sirr."

"Have you had much experience?"

"No that much."

"But you do feel capable of taking on the job?"

"I do, sirr."

"You seem quite eager about it."

"Yes, sirr," said Dunshie, with gusto.

A sudden thought occurred to Ayling.

"Do you know what a chiropodist is?" he asked.

"No, sirr," replied Dunshie, with unabated aplomb.

To do him justice, the revelation of the nature of his prospective labours made no difference whatever to Dunshie's willingness to undertake them. Now, upon Saturday mornings, when men stand stiffly at attention beside their beds to have their feet inspected, you may behold, sweeping majestically in the wake of the Medical Officer as he makes his rounds, the swelling figure of Private Dunshie, carrying the implements of his gruesome trade. He has found his vocation at last, and his bearing in consequence is something between that of a Court Physician and a Staff Officer.

*　　*　　*　　*

So much for the rank and file. Of the officers we need only say that the old hands have been a godsend to our young regiment; while the juniors, to quote their own Colonel, have learned as much in six months as the average subaltern learns in three years; and whereas in the old days a young officer could always depend on his platoon sergeant to give him the right word of command or instruct him in company routine, the positions are now in many cases reversed. But that by the way. The outstanding feature of the relationship between officers and men during all this long, laborious, sometimes heart-breaking winter has been this — that, despite the rawness of our material and the novelty of our surroundings, in the face of difficulties which are now happily growing dim in our memory, the various ranks have never quite given up trying, never altogether lost faith, never entirely forgotten the Cause which has brought us together. And the result — the joint result — of it all is a real live regiment, with a *morale* and soul of its own.

But so far everything has been purely suppositious. We have no knowledge as to what our real strength or weakness may be. We have run our trial trips over a landlocked stretch of smooth water. Tomorrow, when we steam out to face the tempest which is shaking the foundations of the world, we shall see what we shall see. Some of us, who at present are exalted for our smartness and efficiency, will indubitably be found wanting — wanting in stamina of body or soul — while others, hitherto undistinguished, will come to their own. Only War itself can discover the qualities which count in War. But we silently pray, in our dour and inarticulate hearts, that the supreme British virtue — the virtue of holding on, and holding on, and holding on, until our end is accomplished — may not be found wanting in a single one of us.

To take a last survey of the regiment which we have created — one little drop in the incredible wave which has rolled with gathering strength from end to end of this island of ours during the past six months, and now hangs ready to crash upon the gates of our enemies — what manner of man has it produced? What is he like, this impromptu Thomas Atkins?

Well, when he joined, his outstanding feature was a sort of surly independence, the surliness being largely based upon the fear of losing the independence. He has got over that now. He is no longer morbidly sensitive about his rights as a free and independent citizen and the backbone of the British electorate. He has bigger things to think of. He no longer regards sergeants as upstart slave-drivers — frequently he is a sergeant himself — nor officers as grinding capitalists. He is undergoing the experience of the rivets in Mr Kipling's story of *The Ship that Found Herself*. He is adjusting his perspectives. He is beginning to merge himself in the Regiment.

He no longer gets drunk from habit. When he does so now, it is because there were no potatoes at dinner, or because there has been a leak in the roof of his hut for a week and no one is attending to it, or because his wife is not receiving her separation allowance. Being an inarticulate person, he finds getting drunk the simplest and most effective expedient for acquainting the powers that be with the fact that he has a grievance. Formerly, the morning list of "drunks" merely reflected the nearness or remoteness of pay-day. Now, it is a most reliable and invaluable barometer of the regimental atmosphere.

He has developed — quite spontaneously, for he has had few opportunities for imitation — many of the characteristics of the regular soldier. He is quick to discover himself aggrieved, but is readily appeased if he feels that his officer is really doing his best for him, and that both of them are the victims of a higher power. On the other hand, he is often amazingly cheerful under uncomfortable and depressing surroundings. He is growing quite fastidious, too, about his personal appearance when off duty. (You should see our quiffs on Saturdays!) He is quite incapable of keeping possession of his clothing, his boots, his rifle, his health, or anything that is his, without constant supervision and nurse-maiding. And that he is developing a strong bent towards the sentimental is evinced by the choruses that he sings in the gloaming and his taste in picture postcards.

So far he may follow the professional model, but in other respects he is quite *sui generis*. No sergeant in a Highland regiment of the line would ever refer to a Cockney private, with all humility, as "a young English gentleman"; neither would an ordinary soldier salute an officer quite correctly with one hand while employing the other to light his pipe. In "K(1)" we do these things and many others, which give us a *cachet* of our own of which we are very rightly and properly proud.

So we pin our faith to the man who has been at once our despair and our joy since the month of August. He has character; he has grit; and now that he is getting discipline as well, he is going to be an everlasting credit to the cause which roused his manhood and the land which gave him birth.

That is the tale of the First Hundred Thousand — Part One. Whether Part Two will be forthcoming, and how much of it there will be, depends upon two things — the course of history, and the present historian's eye for cover.

BOOK TWO

LIVE ROUNDS

CHAPTER FOURTEEN

THE BACK OF THE FRONT

THE LAST FEW DAYS have afforded us an excellent opportunity of studying the habits of that ubiquitous attendant of our movements, the Staff Officer.

He is not always a real Staff Officer — the kind that wears a red hatband. Sometimes he is an obvious "dugout", with a pronounced *embonpoint* or a game leg. Sometimes he is a mere stripling, with a rapidly increasing size in hats. Sometimes he is an ordinary human being. But whoever he is, and whatever his age or rank, one thing is certain. He has no mean: he is either very good or very bad. When he is good he is very good indeed, and when he is bad he is horrid. He is either Jekyll or Hyde.

Thrice blessed, then, is that unit which, upon its journey to the seat of war, encounters only the good of the species. To transfer a thousand men, with secrecy and despatch, from camp to train, from train to ship, from ship to train, and from train to a spot near the battle line, is a task which calls for the finest organisation and the most skilful administration. Let it be said at once that our path to our present address has been almost universally lined with Jekylls. The few Hydes whom we have encountered are by this time merely a subject for amusing anecdote.

As for the organisation of our journey — well, it was

formulated upon Olympus, and was marked by those Olympian touches of which mention has been previously made. For instance, immense pains were taken, by means of printed rules and official memoranda, to acquaint us with the procedure to be followed at each point of entrainment or embarkation. Consequently we set out upon our complicated pilgrimage primed with explicit instructions and ready for any emergency. We filled up forms with countless details of our equipment and personnel, which we knew would delight the heart of the Round Game Department. We divided our followers, as directed, into Loading Parties, and Ration Parties, and Hold Parties, and many other interesting subdivisions, as required by the rules of the game. But we had reckoned without the Practical Joke Department. The Round Game Department having furnished us with one set of rules, the Practical Joke Department prepared another, entirely different, and issued them to the officers who superintended such things as entrainment and embarkation. At least, that is the most charitable explanation of the course of action adopted by the few Mr Hydes whom we encountered.

Two of these humorists linger in the memory. The first was of the type which is admiringly referred to in commercial circles as a hustler. His hustling took the form of beginning to shout incomprehensible orders almost before the train had drawn up at the platform. After that he passed from party to party, each of which was working strenuously under its own sergeant, and commanded them (not the sergeant) to do something else, somewhere else — a course of action naturally calculated to promote unity and celerity of action all round. A perspiring sergeant who ventured to point out that his party were working under the direct orders of their Company Commander, was promptly placed under arrest, and his flock enjoyed a welcome and protracted breathing-space until an officer of sufficient standing to cope with Mr Hyde — unfortunately he was Major Hyde — could be discovered and informed.

The second required more tactful handling. As our train-load drew up at the platform, the officer in charge — it was Captain Blaikie, supported by Bobby Little — stepped out, saluted the somewhat rotund Colonel Hyde whom he saw before him, and proffered a sheaf of papers.

"Good morning, sir," he said. "Here is my train statement. Shall I carry on with the unloading? I have all my parties detailed."

The great man waved away the papers magnificently. (To be just, even the Jekylls used to wave away our papers.)

"Take those things away," he commanded, in a voice which made it plain that we had encountered another hustler. "Burn them, if you like! Now listen to me. Tell off an officer and seventy men at once."

"I have all the necessary parties detailed already, sir."

"Will you listen to me?" roared the Colonel. He turned to where Captain Blaikie's detachment were drawn up on the platform. "Take the first seventy men of that lot, and tell them to stand over there, under an officer."

Captain Blaikie gave the necessary order.

"Now," continued Colonel Hyde, "tell them to get the horses out and on board that steamer at once. The rest of your party are to go by another steamer. See?"

"Yes, sir, perfectly. But —"

"Do you understand my order?" thundered the Colonel, with increasing choler.

"I do, sir," replied Blaikie politely, "but —"

"Then, for heaven's sake, carry on!"

Blaikie saluted.

"Very good, sir," he answered. "Mr Little, come with me."

He turned upon his heel and disappeared rapidly

round a corner followed by the mystified Bobby.

Once out of the sight of the Colonel, Captain Blaikie halted, leaned against a convenient pillar, and lit a cigarette.

"And what do you think of that?" he inquired.

Bobby told him.

"Quite so," agreed Blaikie. "But what you say helps nobody, though doubtless soothing to the feelings. Now listen, Bobby, and I will give you your first lesson in the Tactical Handling of Brass Hats. Of course we might do as that dear old gentleman suggests, and send seventy horses and mules on a sea voyage in charge of a party of cooks, signallers, and machine-gunners, and let the grooms and drivers go with the bicycles and machine-guns and field kitchens. But I don't think we will. Nobody would enjoy the experiment much — except perhaps the mules. No; we will follow the golden rule, which is: When given an impossible job by a Brass Hat, salute smartly, turn about, and go and wait round a corner for five minutes. Then come back and do the job in a proper manner. Our five minutes are up: the coast should be clear. Come along, Bobby, and help me to exchange these two parties."

But we encountered surprisingly few Hydes. Nearly all were Jekylls — Jekylls of the most competent and courteous type. True, they were inclined to treat our laboriously completed returns with frivolity.

"Never mind those things, old man," they would say. "Just tell me who you are, and how many. That's right: now I know all about you. Got your working parties fixed up? Good! They ought to have everything cleared in a couple of hours. I'll see that a ration of hot tea is served out for them. Your train starts at a quarter past seven this evening — remember to call it nineteen-fifteen, by the way, in this country — and you ought to be at the station an hour before the time. I'll send you a guide. What a fine-looking lot these chaps of yours are!

Best lot I've seen here for a very long time. Working like niggers, too! Now come along with me for ten minutes and I'll show you where to get a bite of breakfast. Expect you can do with a bit!"

That is Brass-Hat Jekyll — officer and gentleman; and, to the eternal credit of the British Army, be it said that he abounds in this well-conducted campaign. As an instance of his efficiency, let the case of our own regiment be quoted. The main body travelled here by one route, the transport, horses, and other details by another. The main body duly landed, and were conveyed to the rendezvous — a distant railway junction in Northern France. There they sat down to await the arrival of the train containing the other party — which had left England many hours before them, had landed at a different port, and had not been seen or heard of since.

They had to wait exactly ten minutes!

"Some Staff — what?" as the Adjutant observed, as the train lumbered into view.

*   *   *   *

Most of us, in our travels abroad, have observed the closed trucks which are employed upon French railways, and which bear the legend —

| *Hommes* | . | . | . | . | . | 40 |
| *Chevaux* | . | . | . | . | . | 8 |

Doubtless we have wondered, idly enough, what it must feel like to be one of the forty *hommes*. Well, now we know.

When we landed, we were packed into a train composed of fifty such trucks, and were drawn by a mighty engine for a day and a night across the pleasant land of France. Every six hours or so we were indulged with a *Halte Répas*. That is to say, the train drew up in a siding, where an officer with R.T.O. upon his arm made us welcome, and informed us that hot water was available for making tea. Everybody had two days' rations in his haversack, so a large-scale picnic followed. From the horse-trucks emerged stolid individuals with canvas buckets — you require to be fairly stolid to pass the night in a closed box, moving at twenty miles an hour, in company with eight riotous and insecurely tethered mules — to draw water from the hydrant which supplied the locomotives. The infant population gathered round, and besought us for "souvenirs", the most popular taking the form of "biskeet" or "bully-bœuf". Both were given freely: with but little persuasion our open-handed warriors would have fain squandered their sacred "emergency ration" upon these rapacious infants.

After refreshment we proceeded to inspect the station. The centre of attraction was the French soldier on guard over the water-tank. Behold this same sentry confronted by Private Mucklewame, anxious to comply with Divisional Orders and "lose no opportunity of cultivating the friendliest relations with those of our Allies whom you may chance to encounter." So Mucklewame and the sentry (who is evidently burdened with similar instructions) regard one another with shy smiles, after the fashion of two children who have been introduced by their nurses at a party.

Presently the sentry, by a happy inspiration, proffers his bayonet for inspection, as it were a new doll. Mucklewame bows solemnly, and fingers the blade. Then he produces his own bayonet, and the two weapons are compared — still in constrained silence. Then Mucklewame nods approvingly.

"Verra goody!" he remarks, profoundly convinced that he is speaking the French language.

"Olrigh! Tipperaree!" replies the sentry, not to be outdone in international courtesy.

Unfortunately, the further cementing of the Entente Cordiale is frustrated by the blast of a whistle. We hurl ourselves into our trucks; the R.T.O. waves his hand in benediction; and the regiment proceeds upon its way, packed like herrings, but "all jubilant with song".

*   *   *   *

We have been "oot here" for a week now, and although we have had no personal encounter with the foe, our time has not been wasted. We are filling up gaps in our education, and we are tolerably busy. Some things, of course, we have not had to learn. We are fairly well inured, for instance, to hard work and irregular meals. What we have chiefly to acquire at present is the art of adaptability. When we are able to settle down into strange billets in half an hour, and pack up, ready for departure, within the same period, we shall have made a great stride in efficiency, and added enormously to our own personal comfort.

Even now we are making progress. Observe the platoon who are marching into this farmyard. They are dead tired, and the sight of the straw-filled barn is too much for some of them. They throw themselves down anywhere, and are asleep in a moment. When they wake up — or more likely, are wakened up — in an hour or two, they will be sorry. They will be stiff and sore, and their feet will be torment. Other, more sensible, crowd round the pump, or dabble their abraded extremities in one of the countless ditches with which this country is intersected. Others again, of the more enterprising kind, repair to the house door, and inquire politely for "the wife". (They have long given up inquiring for "the master". There is no master on this farm, or indeed on any farm throughout the length and breadth of this great-hearted land. Father and sons are all away, restoring the Boche to his proper place in the animal kingdom. We have seen no young or middle-aged man out of uniform since we entered this district, save an occasional imbecile or cripple.)

Presently "the wife" comes to the door, with a smile. She can afford to smile now, for not so long ago her guests were Uhlans. Then begins an elaborate panto-mime. Private Tosh says "Bonjourr!" in husky tones — last week he would have said "Hey, Bella!" — and pro-ceeds to wash his hands in invisible soap and water. As a reward for his ingenuity he receives a basin of water: sometimes the water is even warm. Meanwhile Private Cosh the linguist of the platoon, proffers twopence, and says: "Doolay — ye unnerstand?" He gets a drink of milk, which is a far, far better thing than the appalling green scum-covered water with which his less adapt-able brethren are wont to refresh themselves from wayside ditches. Thomas Atkins, however mature, is quite incorrigible in this respect.

Yes, we are getting on. And when every man in the platoon, instead of merely some, can find a place to sleep, draw his blanket from the waggon, clean his rifle and himself, and get to his dinner within the half-hour already specified, we shall be able justly to call our-selves seasoned.

We have covered some distance this week, and we have learned one thing at last, and that is, not to be uppish about our sleeping quarters. We have slept in chateaux, convents, farm-houses, and under the open sky. The chateaux are usually empty. An aged retainer, the sole inhabitant, explains that M. le Comte is at Paris; M. Armand at Arras; and M. Guy in Alsace — all doing their bit. M. Victor is in hospital, with Madame and Mademoiselle in constant attendance.

So we settle down in the chateau, and unroll our sleeping-bags upon its dusty parquet. Occasionally we find a bed available. Then two officers take the mattress, upon the floor, and two more take what is left of the bed. French chateaux do not appear to differ much as a class. They are distinguished by great elegance of design, infinite variety in furniture, and entire absence of drains. The same rule applies to convents, except that there is no furniture.

Given fine weather, by far the most luxurious form of lodging is in the open air. Here one may slumber at ease, fanned by the wings of cockchafers and soothed by an unseen choir of frogs. There are drawbacks, of course. Mr Waddell one evening spread his ground-sheet and bedding in the grassy meadow, beside a murmuring stream. It was an idyllic resting-place for a person of romantic or contemplative disposition. Unfortunately it is almost impossible nowadays to keep one's favourite haunts select. This was evidently the opinion of the large water-rat which Waddell found sitting upon his air-pillow when he returned from supper. Although French, the animal exhibited no disposition to fraternise, but withdrew in the most pointed fashion, taking an Abernethy biscuit with him.

Accommodation in farms is best described by the word "promiscuous". There are twelve officers and two hundred men billeted here. The farm is exactly the same as any other French farm. It consists of a hollow square of buildings — dwelling-house, barns, pigstyes, and stables — with a commodious manure-heap, occupying the whole yard except a narrow strip round the edge, in the middle, the happy hunting-ground of innumerable cocks and hens and an occasional pig. The men sleep in the barns. The senior officers sleep in a stone-floored boudoir of their own. The juniors sleep where they can, and experience little difficulty in accomplishing the feat. A hard day's marching and a truss of straw — these two combined form an irresistible inducement to slumber.

Only a few miles away big guns thunder until the

building shakes. Tomorrow a select party of officers is to pay a visit to the trenches. Thereafter our whole flock is to go, in its official capacity. The War is with us at last. Early this morning a Zeppelin rose into view on the skyline. Shell fire pursued it, and it sank again — rumour says in the British lines. Rumour is our only war correspondent at present. It is far easier to follow the course of events from home, where newspapers are more plentiful than here.

But the grim realities of war are coming home to us. Outside this farm stands a tall tree. Not many months ago a party of Uhlans arrived here, bringing with them a wounded British prisoner. They crucified him to that self-same tree, and stood round him till he died. He was a long time dying.

Some of us had not heard of Uhlans before. These have now noted the name, for future reference — and action.

CHAPTER FIFTEEN

IN THE TRENCHES —
AN OFF-DAY

THIS TOWN is under constant shell fire. It goes on day after day: it has been going on for months. Sometimes a single shell comes: sometimes half a dozen. Sometimes whole batteries get to work. The effect is terrible. You who live at home in ease have no conception of what it is like to live in a town which is under intermittent shell fire.

I say this advisedly. You have no conception whatso-ever.

We get no rest. There is a distant boom, followed by a crash overhead. Cries are heard — the cries of women and children. They are running frantically — running to observe the explosion, and if possible pick up a piece of the shell as a souvenir. Sometimes there are not enough souvenirs to go round, and then the clamour increases.

We get no rest, I say — only frightfulness. British officers, walking peaceably along the pavement, are frequently hustled and knocked aside by these persons. Only the other day, a full colonel was compelled to turn up a side-street, to avoid disturbing a ring of excited children who were dancing round a beautiful new hole in the ground in the middle of a narrow lane.

If you enter into a café or estaminet, a total stranger

sidles to your table, and, having sat down beside you, produces from the recesses of his person a fragment of shrapnel. This he lays before you, and explains that if he had been standing at the spot where the shell burst, it would have killed him. You express polite regret, and pass on elsewhere, seeking peace and finding none. The whole thing is a public scandal.

Seriously, though, it is astonishing what contempt familiarity can breed, even in the case of high-explosive shells. This little town lies close behind the trenches. All day long the big guns boom. By night the rifles and machine-guns take up the tale. One is frequently aroused from slumber, especially towards dawn, by a perfect tornado of firing. The machine-guns make a noise like a giant tearing calico. Periodically, too, as already stated, we are subjected to an hour's intimidation in the shape of bombardment. Shrapnel bursts over our heads; shells explode in the streets, especially in open spaces, or where two important streets cross. (With modern artillery you can shell a town quite methodically by map and compass.)

Brother Boche's motto appears to be: "It is a fine morning. There is nothing in the trenches doing. We abundant ammunition have. Let us a little frightfulness into the town pump!" So he pumps.

But nobody seems to mind. Of course there is a casualty now and then. Occasionally a hole is blown in a road, or the side of a house is knocked in. Yet the general attitude of the population is one of rather interested expectancy. There is always the cellar to retire to if things get really serious. The gratings are sandbagged to that end. At other times — well, there is always the pleasing possibility of witnessing the sudden removal of your neighbour's landmark.

Officers breakfasting in their billets look up from their porridge, and say —

"That's a dud! *That's* a better one! Stick to it, Bill!"

It really is most discouraging, to a sensitive and conscientious Hun.

The same unconcern reigns in the trenches. Let us imagine that we are members of a distinguished party from Headquarters, about to make a tour of inspection.

We leave the town, and after a short walk along the inevitable poplar-lined road turn into a field. The country all around us is flat — flat as Cheshire; and, like Cheshire, has a pond in every field. But in the hazy distance stands a low ridge.

"Better keep close to the hedge," suggests the officer in charge. "There are eighty guns on that ridge. It's a misty morning; but they've got all the ranges about here to a yard; so they *might* —"

We keep close to the hedge.

Presently we find ourselves entering upon a wide but sticky path cut in the clay. At the entrance stands a neat notice-board, which announces somewhat unexpectedly:

OLD KENT ROAD

The field is flat, but the path runs downhill. Consequently we soon find ourselves tramping along below the ground-level, with a stout parapet of clay on either side of us. Overhead there is nothing — nothing but the blue sky, with the larks singing, quite regardless of the War.

"Communication trench," explains the guide.

We tramp along this sunken lane for the best part of a mile. It winds a good deal. Every hundred yards or so comes a great promontory of sandbags, necessitating four right-angle turns. Once we pass under the shadow of trees, and apple-blossom flutters down upon our upturned faces. We are walking through an orchard. Despite the efforts of ten million armed men, brown old Mother Earth has made it plain that seed–time and harvest shall still prevail.

Now we are crossing a stream, which cuts the trench at right angles. The stream is spanned by a structure of planks — labelled, it is hardly necessary to say, LONDON BRIDGE. The sidestreet, so to speak, by which the stream runs away is called JOCK'S JOY. We ask why?

"It's the place where the Highlanders wash their knees," is the explanation.

Presently we arrive at PICCADILLY CIRCUS, a muddy excavation in the earth, from which several passages branch. These thoroughfares are not all labelled with strict regard for London geography. We note THE HAYMARKET, also PICCADILLY; but ARTILLERY LANE seems out of place, somehow. On the site, too, of the Criterion, we observe a subterranean cavern containing three recumbent figures, snoring lustily. This bears the sign CYCLISTS' REST.

We, however, take the turning marked SHAFTESBURY AVENUE, and after passing (quite wrongly, don't you think?) through TRAFALGAR SQUARE — six feet by eight — find ourselves in the actual firing trench.

It is an unexpectedly spacious place. We, who have spent the winter constructing slits in the ground two feet wide, feel quite lost in this roomy thoroughfare. For a thoroughfare it is, with little toy houses on either side. They are hewn out of the solid earth, lined with planks, painted, furnished, and decorated. These are, so to speak, permanent trenches, which have been occupied for more than six months.

Observe this eligible residence on your left. It has a little door, nearly six feet high, and a real glass window, with a little curtain. Inside, there is a bunk, six feet long, together with an ingenious folding washhand-stand, of the nautical variety, and a flap-table. The walls, which are painted pale green, are decorated with elegant extracts from *The Sketch* and *La Vie Parisienne*.

Outside, the name of the villa is painted up. It is in Welsh — that notorious railway station in Anglesey which runs to thirty-three syllables or so — and extends from one end of the façade to the other. A small placard announces that Hawkers, Organs, and Street-cries are prohibited.

"This is my shanty," explains a machine-gun officer standing by. "It was built by a Welsh Fusilier, who has since moved on. He was here all winter, and made everything himself, including the washhand-stand. Some carpenter — what? of course I am not here continuously. We have six days in the trenches and six out; so I take turns with a man in the Midland Mudcrushers, who take turns with us. Come in and have some tea."

It is only ten o'clock in the morning, but tea — strong and sweet, with condensed milk — is instantly forthcoming. Refreshed by this, and a slice of cake, we proceed upon our excursion.

The trench is full of men, mostly asleep; for the night cometh, when no man may sleep. They lie in low-roofed rectangular caves, like the interior of great cucumber-frames, lined with planks and supported by props. The cave is really a homogeneous affair, for it is constructed in R.E. workshops and then brought bodily to the trenches and fitted into its appointed excavation. Each cave holds three men. They lie side by side, like three dogs in a triple kennel, with their heads outward and easily accessible to the individual who performs the functions of "knocker-up".

Others are cooking, others are cleaning their rifles. The proceedings are superintended by a contemplative tabby cat, coiled up in a niche, like a feline flower in a crannied wall.

"She used ter sit on top of the parapet," explains a friendly lance-corporal; "but became a casualty, owin' to a sniper mistakin' 'er for a Guardsman's bearskin. Show the officer your back, Christabel!"

We inspect the healed scar, and pass on. Next moment we round a traverse — and walk straight into the arms of Privates Ogg and Hogg!

No need now to remain with the distinguished party from Headquarters. For the next half-mile of trench you will find yourselves among friends. "K(1)" and Brother Boche are face to face at last, and here you behold our own particular band of warriors taking their first spell in the trenches.

Let us open the door of this spacious dug-out — the image of an up-river bungalow, decorated with window-boxes and labelled POTSDAM VIEW — and join the party of four which sits round the table.

"How did your fellows get on last night, Wagstaffe?" inquires Major Kemp.

"Very well, on the whole. It was a really happy thought on the part of the authorities — almost human, in fact — to put us in alongside the old regiment."

"Or what's left of them."

Wagstaffe nods gravely.

"Yes. There are some changes in the Mess since I last dined there," he says. "Anyhow, the old hands took our boys to their bosoms at once, and showed them the ropes."

"The men did not altogether fancy look-out work in the dark, sir," says Bobby Little to Major Kemp.

"Neither should I, very much," said Kemp. "To take one's stand on a ledge fixed at a height which brings one's head and shoulders well above the parapet, and stand there for an hour on end, knowing that a machine-gun may start a spell of rapid traversing fire at any moment — well, it takes a bit of doing, you know, until you are used to it. How did you persuade 'em, Bobby?"

"Oh, I just climbed up on the top of the parapet and sat there for a bit," says Bobby Little modestly. "They were all right after that."

"Had you any excitement, Ayling?" asks Kemp. "I hear rumours that you had two casualties."

"Yes," says Ayling. "Four of us went out patrolling in front of the trench —"

"Who?"

"Myself, two men, and old Sergeant Carfrae."

"Carfrae?" Wagstaffe laughs. "That old fire-eater? I remember him at Paardeberg. You were lucky to get back alive. Proceed, my son!"

"We went out," continues Ayling, "and patrolled".

"How?"

"Well, there you rather have me. I have always been a bit foggy as to what a patrol really does — what risks it takes, and so on. However, Carfrae had no doubts on the subject whatever. His idea was to trot over to the German trenches and look inside."

"Quite so!" agreed Wagstaffe, and Kemp chuckled.

"Well, we were standing by the barbed-wire entanglement, arguing the point, when suddenly some infernal imbecile in our own trenches —"

"Cockerell, for a dollar!" murmurs Wagstaffe. "Don't say he fired at you!"

"No, he did worse. He let off a fire-ball."

"Whew! And there you stood in the limelight!"

"Exactly."

"What did you do?"

"I had sufficient presence of mind to do what Carfrae did. I threw myself on my face, and shouted to the two men to do the same."

"Did they?"

"No. They started to run back towards the trenches. Half a dozen German rifles opened on them at once."

"Were they badly hit?"

"Nothing to speak of, considering. The shots mostly went high. Preston got his elbow smashed, and Burke had a bullet through his cap and another in the region of the waistband. Then they tumbled into the trench like rabbits. Carfrae and I crawled after them."

At this moment the doorway of the dug-out is darkened by a massive figure, and Major Kemp's colour-sergeant announces —

"There's a parrty of Gairmans gotten oot o' their trenches, sirr. Will we open fire?"

"Go and have a look at 'em, like a good chap, Wagger," says the Major. "I want to finish this letter."

Wagstaffe and Bobby Little make their way along the trench until they come to a low opening marked MAXIM VILLA. They crawl inside, and find themselves in a semicircular recess, chiefly occupied by an earthen platform, upon which a machine-gun is mounted. The recess is roofed over, heavily protected with sandbags, and lined with iron plates; for a machine-gun emplacement is the object of frequent and pressing attention from high-explosive shells. There are loopholes to right and left, but not in front. These deadly weapons prefer diagonal or enfilade fire. It is not worth while to fire them frontally.

Wagstaffe draws back a strip of sacking which covers one loophole, and peers out. There, a hundred and fifty yards away, across a sunlit field, he beholds some twenty grey figures, engaged in the most pastoral of pursuits, in front of the German trenches.

"They are cutting the grass," he says. "Let 'em, by all means! If they don't, we must. We don't want their bomb-throwers crawling over here through a hayfield. Let us encourage them by every means in our power. It might almost be worth our while to send them a message. Walk along the trench, Bobby, and see that no excitable person looses off at them."

Bobby obeys; and peace still broods over the sleepy trench. The only sound which breaks the summer stillness is the everlasting crack, crack! of the snipers' rifles. On an off-day like this the sniper is a very necessary person. He serves to remind us that we are at war. Concealed in his particular eyrie, with his eyes for ever laid along his telescopic sight, he keeps ceaseless vigil over the ragged outline of the enemy's trenches. Wherever a head, or anything resembling a head, shows itself, he fires. Were it not for his enthusiasm, both sides would be sitting in their shirt-sleeves upon their respective parapets, regarding one another with frank curiosity; and that would never do. So the day wears on.

Suddenly, from far in our rear, comes a boom, then another. Wagstaffe sighs resignedly.

"Why can't they let well alone?" he complains. "What's the trouble now?"

"I expect it's our Divisional Artillery having a little target practice," says Captain Blaikie. He peers into a neighbouring trench-periscope. "Yes, they are shelling that farm behind the German second-line trench. Making good shooting too, for beginners," as a column of dust and smoke rises from behind the enemy lines. "But brother Boche will be very peevish about it. We don't usually fire at this time of the afternoon. Yes, there is the haymaking party going home. There will be a beastly noise for the next half-hour. Pass the word along for every man to get into his dug-out."

The warning comes none too soon. In five minutes the incensed Hun is retaliating for the disturbance of his afternoon siesta. A hail of bullets passes over our trench. Shrapnel bursts overhead. High-explosive shells rain upon and around the parapet. One drops into the trench, and explodes, with surprisingly little effect. (Bobby Little found the head afterwards, and sent it home as a memento of his first encounter with reality.)

Our trench makes no reply. There is no need. This outburst heralds no grand assault. It is a mere display of "frightfulness", calculated to cow the impressionable Briton. We sit close, and make tea. Only the look-out men, crouching behind their periscopes and loopholes, keep their posts. The wind is the wrong way for gas, and in any case we all have respirators. Private McLeary, the humorist of A Company, puts his on, and pretends to drink his tea through it.

Altogether, the British soldier appears sadly unappreciative either of "frightfulness" or practical chemistry. He is a hopeless case.

The firing ceases as suddenly as it began. Silence reigns again, broken only by a solitary shot from a trench-mortar — a sort of explosive postscript to a half-hour's Hymn of Hate.

"And that's that!" observes Captain Blaikie cheerfully, emerging from Potsdam View. "The Hun is a harmless little creature, but noisy when roused. Now, what about getting home? It will be dark in half an hour or so. Platoon commanders, warn your men!"

It should be noted that upon this occasion we are not doing our full spell of duty — that is, six days. We have merely come in for a spell of instruction, of twenty-four hours' duration, under the chaperonage of our elder and more seasoned brethren.

Bobby Little, having given the necessary orders to his sergeant, proceeded to Trafalgar Square, there to await the mustering of his platoon.

But the first arrival took the form of a slow-moving procession — a corporal, followed by two men carrying a stretcher. On the stretcher lay something covered with a ground-sheet. At one end projected a pair of regulation boots, very still and rigid.

Bobby caught his breath. He was just nineteen, and this was his first encounter with sudden death.

"Who is it?" he asked unsteadily.

The corporal saluted.

"Private McLeary, sirr. That last shot from the trench-mortar got him. It came in kin' o' sideways. He was sittin' at the end of his dug-out, gettin' his tea. Stretcher party, advance!"

The procession moved off again, and disappeared round the curve of Shaftesbury Avenue. The off-day was over.

CHAPTER SIXTEEN

"DIRTY WORK AT THE CROSS-ROADS TONIGHT"

LAST WEEK we abandoned the rural billets in which we had been remodelling some of our methods (on the experiences gained by our first visit to the trenches), and paraded at full strength for a march which we knew would bring us right into the heart of things. No more trial trips; no more chaperoning! This time, we decided, we were "for it".

During our three weeks of active service we have learned two things — the art of shaking down quickly into our habitation of the moment, as already noted; and the art of reducing our personal effects to a portable minimum.

To the private soldier the latter problem presents no difficulties. Everything is arranged for him. His outfit is provided by the Government, and he carries it himself. It consists of a rifle, bayonet, and a hundred and twenty rounds of ammunition. On one side of him hangs his water-bottle, containing a quart of water, on the other, a haversack, occupied by his "iron ration" — an emergency meal of the tinned variety, which must never on any account be opened except by order of the C.O. — and such private effects as his smoking outfit and an entirely mythical item of refreshment officially known as "the unexpended portion of the day's ration". On his back he carries a "pack", containing his greatcoat, waterproof sheet, and such changes of raiment as a paternal Government allows him. He also has to find room therein for a towel, housewife, and a modest allowance of cutlery. (He frequently wears the spoon in his stocking as a skean-dhu.) Round his neck he wears his identity disc. In his breast-pocket he carries a respirator, to be donned in the event of his encountering the twin misfortunes of an east wind and a gaseous Hun. He also carries a bottle of liquid for damping the respirator. In the flap of his jacket is sewn a field dressing.

Slung behind him is an entrenching tool.

Any other space upon his person is at his own disposal, and he may carry what he likes, except "unsoldierly trinkets" — whatever these may be. However, if the passion for self-adornment proves too strong, he may wear "the French National colours" — a compliment to our gallant ally which is slightly discounted by the fact that her national colours are the same as our own.

However, once he has attached this outfit to his suffering person, and has said what he thinks about its weight, the private has no more baggage worries. Except for his blanket, which is carried on a waggon, he is his own arsenal, wardrobe, and pantry.

Not so the officer. He suffers from *embarras de choix*. He is the victim of his female relatives, who are themselves the victims of those enterprising tradesmen who have adopted the most obvious method of getting rid of otherwise unsaleable goods by labelling everything *For Active Service* — a really happy thought when you are trying to sell a pipe of port or a manicure set. Have you seen Our Active Service Trouser Press?

By the end of April Bobby Little had accumulated, with a view to facilitating the destruction of the foe —

An automatic Mauser pistol, with two thousand rounds of ammunition.

A regulation Service revolver.

A camp bed.

A camp table.

A camp chair.

A pneumatic mattress.

[This ingenious contrivance was meant to be blown up, like an air-cushion, and Bobby's servant expended most of the day and much valuable breath in performing the feat. Ultimately, in a misguided attempt to save his lungs from rupture, he employed a bicycle pump, and burst the bed.]

A sleeping (or "flea") bag.

A portable bath.

A portable washhand-stand.

A dressing-case, heavily ballasted with cut-glass bottles.

A primus stove.

A despatch case.

The "Service" Kipling. (About forty volumes.)

Innumerable socks and shirts.

A box of soap.

Fifty boxes of matches.

A small medicine chest.

About a dozen first-aid outfits.

A case of pipes, and cigarettes innumerable.

[Bobby's aunts regarded cigars as not quite ascetic enough for active service. Besides, they might make him sick.]

About a cubic foot of chocolate (various).

Numerous compressed foods and concentrated drinks.

An "active service" cooking outfit.

An electric lamp, with several refills.

A pair of binoculars.

A telescope.

A prismatic compass.

A sparklet siphon.

A luminous watch.

A pair of insulated wire-cutters.

"There's only one thing you've forgotten," remarked Captain Wagstaffe, when introduced to this unique collection of curios.

"What is that?" inquired Bobby, always eager to learn.

"A pantechnicon! Do you know how much personal baggage an officer is allowed, in addition to what he carries himself?"

"Thirty-five pounds."

"Correct."

"It sounds a lot," said Bobby.

"It looks precious little!" was Wagstaffe's reply.

"I suppose they won't be particular to a pound or so," said Bobby optimistically.

"Listen," commanded Wagstaffe. "When we go abroad, your Wolseley valise, containing this" — he swept his hand round the crowded hut — "this military museum, will be handed to the Quartermaster. He is a man of singularly rigid mind, with an exasperating habit of interpreting rules and regulations quite literally. If you persist in this scheme of asking him to pass half a ton of assorted lumber as a package weighing thirty-five pounds, he will cast you forth and remain your enemy for life. And personally," concluded Wagstaffe, "I would rather keep on the right side of my Regimental Quartermaster than of the Commander-in-Chief himself. Now, send all this stuff home — you can use it on manoeuvres in peace-time — and I will give you a little list which will not break the baggage-waggon's back."

The methodical Bobby produced a note-book.

"You will require to wash occasionally. Take a canvas bucket, some carbolic soap, and a good big towel. Also your toothbrush, and — excuse the question, but do you shave?"

"Twice a week", admitted the blushing Bobby.

"Happy man! Well, take a safety-razor. That will do for cleanliness. Now for clothing. Lots of socks, but only one change of other things, unless you care to take a third shirt in your greatcoat pocket. Two good pairs of boots, and a pair of slacks. Then, as regards sleeping. Your flea-bag and your three Government blankets, with your valise underneath, will keep you (and your little bedfellows) as warm as toast. You may get separated from your valise, though, so take a ground-sheet in your pack. Then you will be ready to dine and sleep simply anywhere, at a moment's notice. As regards comforts generally, take a 'Tommy's cooker', if you can find room for it, and scrap all the rest of your cuisine except your canteen. Take a few meat lozenges and some chocolate in one of your ammunition pouches, in case you ever have to go without your breakfast. Rotten work, marching or fighting on a hollow tummy!"

"What about revolvers?" inquired Bobby, displaying his arsenal, a little nervously.

"If the Germans catch you with that Mauser, they will hang you. Take the Webley. Then you can always draw Service ammunition." Wagstaffe ran his eye over the rest of Bobby's outfit. "Smokes? Take your pipe and a tinder-box: you will get baccy and cigarettes to burn out there. Keep that electric torch; and your binoculars, of course. Also that small map-case: it's a good one. Also wire-cutters. You can write letters in your field-message-book. Your compass is all right. Add a pair of canvas shoes — they're a godsend after a long day, — an air-pillow, some candle-ends, a tin of vaseline, and a ball of string, and I think you will do. If you find you still have a pound or so in hand, add a few books — something to fall back on, in case supplies fail. Personally, I'm taking *Vanity Fair* and *Pickwick*. But then, I'm old-fashioned."

Bobby took Wagstaffe's advice, with the result that

that genial obstructionist, the Quartermaster, smiled quite benignly upon him when he presented his valise; while his brother officers, sternly bidden to revise their equipment, were compelled at the last moment to discriminate frantically between the claims of necessity and luxury — often disastrously.

However, we had all found our feet, and developed into seasoned vagabonds when we set out for the trenches last week. A few days previously we had been inspected by Sir John French himself.

"And that," explained Major Kemp to his subalterns, "usually means dirty work at the cross-roads at no very distant period!"

Major Kemp was right — quite literally right.

Our march took us back to Armentières, whose sufferings under intermittent shell fire have already been described. We marched by night, and arrived at breakfast-time. The same evening two companies and a section of machine-gunners were bidden to equip themselves with picks and shovels and parade at dusk. An hour later we found ourselves proceeding cautiously along a murky road close behind the trenches.

The big guns were silent, but the snipers were busy on both sides. A German searchlight was combing out the heavens above: a constant succession of star-shells illumined the earth beneath.

"What are we going to do tonight, sir?" inquired Bobby Little, heroically resisting an inclination to duck, as a Mauser bullet spat viciously over his head.

"I believe we are going to dig a redoubt behind the trenches," replied Captain Blaikie. "I expect to meet an R.E. officer somewhere about here, and he will tell us the worst. That was a fairly close one, Bobby! Pass the word down quietly that the men are to keep in to each side of the road, and walk as low as they can. Ah, there is our sportsman, I fancy. Good evening!"

A subaltern of that wonderful corps, the Royal Engineers, loomed out of the darkness, removed a cigarette from his mouth, and saluted politely.

"Good evening, sir," he said to Blaikie. "Will you follow me, please? I have marked out each man's digging position with white tape, so they ought to find no difficulty in getting to work. Brought your machine-gun officer?"

The machine-gun officer, Ayling, was called up.

"We are digging a sort of square fort," explained the Engineer, "to hold a battalion. That will mean four guns to mount. I don't know much about machine-guns myself; so perhaps you" — to Ayling — "will walk round with me outside the position, and you can select your own emplacements."

"I shall be charmed," replied Ayling, and Blaikie chuckled.

"I'll just get your infantry to work first," continued the phlegmatic youth. "This way, sir!"

The road at this point ran through a hollow square of trees, and it was explained to the working party that the trees, roughly, followed the outlines of the redoubt.

"The trenches are about half-finished," added the Engineer. "We had a party from the Seaforths working here last night. Your men have only to carry on where they left off. It's chiefly a matter of filling sandbags and placing them on the parapet." He pointed to a blurred heap in a corner of the wood. "There are fifty thousand there. Leave what you don't want!"

"Where do we get the earth to fill the sandbags?" asked Blaikie. "The trenches, or the middle of the redoubt?"

"Oh, pretty well anywhere," replied the Engineer. "Only, warn your men to be careful not to dig too deep!"

And with this dark saying he lounged off to take

Ayling for his promised walk.

"I'll take you along the road a bit, first," he said, "and then we will turn off into the field where the corner of the redoubt is, and you can look at things from the outside."

Ayling thanked him, and stepped somewhat higher than usual, as a bullet struck the ground at his feet.

"Extraordinary how few casualties one gets," continued the Sapper chattily. "Their snipers go potting away all night, but they don't often get anybody. By the way, they have a machine-gun trained on this road, but they only loose it off every second night. Methodical beggars!"

"Did they loose it off last night?"

"No. Tonight's the night. Have you finished here?"

"Yes, thanks!"

"Right-o! We'll go to the next corner. You'll get a first-class field of fire there, I should say."

The second position was duly inspected, the only incident of interest being the bursting of a star-shell directly overhead.

"Better lie down for a minute," suggested the Engineer.

Ayling, who had been struggling with a strong inclination to do so for some time, promptly complied.

"Just like the Crystal Palace on a benefit night!" observed his guide admiringly, as the landscape was lit up with a white glare. "Now you can see your position beautifully. You can fire obliquely in this direction, and then do a first-class enfilade if the trenches get rushed."

"I see," said Ayling, surveying the position with real interest. He was beginning to enjoy selecting gun-emplacements which really mattered. It was a change from nine months of "eye-wash".

When the German star-shell had spent itself they crossed the road, to the rear of the redoubt, and marked the other two emplacements — in comparative safety now.

"The only trouble about this place," said Ayling, as he surveyed the last position, "is that my fire will be masked by that house with the clump of trees beside it."

The Engineer produced a small note-book, and wrote in it by the light of a convenient star-shell.

"Right-o!" he said. "I'll have the whole caboodle pushed over for you by tomorrow night. Anything else?"

Ayling began to enjoy himself. After you have spent nine months in an unprofitable attempt to combine practical machine-gun tactics with a scrupulous respect for private property, the realisation that you may now gratify your destructive instincts to the full comes as a welcome and luxurious shock.

"Thanks," he said. "You might flatten out that hay-stack, too."

They found the others hard at work when they returned. Captain Blaikie was directing operations from the centre of the redoubt.

"I say," he said, as the Engineer sat down beside him, "I'm afraid we're doing a good deal of body-snatching. This place is absolutely full of little wooden crosses."

"Germans," replied the Engineer laconically.

"How long have they been — here?"

"Since October."

"So I should imagine," said Blaikie, with feeling.

"The crosses aren't much guide, either," continued the Engineer. "The deceased are simply all over the place. The best plan is to dig until you come to a blan-ket. (There are usually two or three to a blanket.) Then tell off a man to flatten down clay over the place at once, and try somewhere else. It is a rotten job, though, however you look at it."

"Have you been here long?" inquired Bobby Little,

who had come across the road for a change of air.

"Long enough! But I'm not on duty continuously. I am Box. Cox takes over tomorrow." He rose to his feet and looked at his watch.

"You ought to move off by half-past one, sir," he said to Blaikie. "It begins to get light after that, and the Boches have three shells for that cross-road over there down in their time-table at two-fifteen. They're a hide-bound lot, but punctual!"

"Thanks," said Blaikie. "I shall not neglect your advice. It is half-past eleven now. Come along, Bobby, and we'll see how old Ayling is getting on."

Steadily, hour by hour, in absolute silence, the work went on. There was no talking, but (under extenuating circumstances) smoking was permitted. Periodically, as the star-shells burst into brilliance overhead, the workers sank down behind a parapet, or, if there was no time, stood rigid — the one thing to avoid upon these occasions is movement of any kind — and gave the snipers a chance. It was not pleasant, but it was duty; and the word duty has become a mighty force in "K(1)" these days. No one was hit, which was remarkable, when you consider what an artist a German sniper is. Possibly the light of the star-shells was deceptive, or possibly there is some truth in the general rumour that the Saxons, who hold this part of the line, are well-disposed towards us, and conduct their offensive operations with a tactful blend of constant firing and bad shooting, which, while it satisfies the Prussians, causes no serious inconvenience to Thomas Atkins.

At a quarter-past one a subdued order ran round the trenches; the men fell in on the sheltered side of the plantation; picks and shovels were checked; rifles and equipment were resumed; and the party stole silently away to the cross-road, where the three shells were timed to arrive at two-fifteen. When they did so, with true Teutonic punctuality, an hour later, our friends were well on their way home to billets and bed — with the dawn breaking behind them, the larks getting to work overhead, and all the infected air of the German graveyard swept out of their lungs by the dew of the morning.

As for that imperturbable philosopher, Box, he sat down with a cigarette, and waited for Cox.

CHAPTER SEVENTEEN

THE NEW WARFARE

THE TRENCH SYSTEM has one thing to recommend it. It tidies things up.

For the first few months after the war broke out confusion reigned supreme. Belgium and the north of France were one huge jumbled battlefield, rather like a public park on a Saturday afternoon — one of those parks where promiscuous football is permitted. Friend and foe were inextricably mingled, and the direction of the goal was uncertain. If you rode into a village, you might find it occupied by a Highland regiment or a squadron of Uhlans. If you dimly discerned troops marching side by side with you in the dawning, it was by no means certain that they would prove to be your friends. On the other hand, it was never safe to assume that a battalion which you saw hastily entrenching itself against your approach was German. It might belong to your own brigade. There was no front and no rear, so direction counted for nothing. The country swarmed with troops which had been left "in the air", owing to their own too rapid advance, or the equally rapid retirement of their supporters; with scattered details trying to rejoin their units; or with despatch-riders hunting for a peripatetic Divisional Headquarters. Snipers shot both sides impartially. It was all most upsetting.

Well, as already indicated, the trench system had put all that right. The trenches now run continuously — a long, irregular, but perfectly definite line of cleavage — from the North Sea to the Vosges. Everybody has been carefully sorted out — human beings on one side, Germans on the other. ("Like the Zoo," observes Captain Wagstaffe.) Nothing could be more suitable. *You're there, and I'm here, so what do we care?* in fact.

The result is an agreeable blend of war and peace. This week, for instance, our battalion has been undergoing a sort of rest-cure a few miles from the hottest part of the firing line. (We had a fairly heavy spell of work last week.) In the morning we wash our clothes, and perform a few mild martial exercises. In the afternoon we sleep, in all degrees of *déshabille,* under the trees in an orchard. In the evening we play football, or bathe in the canal, or lie on our backs on the grass, watching our aeroplanes buzzing home to roost, attended by German shrapnel. We could not have done this in the autumn. Now, thanks to our trenches, a few miles away, we are as safe here as in the wilds of Argyllshire or West Kensington.

But there are drawbacks to everything. The fact is, a trench is that most uninteresting of human devices, a compromise. It is neither satisfactory as a domicile nor efficient as a weapon of offence. The most luxuriant dug-out; the most artistic window-box — these, in spite of all biassed assertions to the contrary, compare unfavourably with a flat in Knightsbridge. On the other hand, the knowledge that you are keeping yourself tolerably immune from the assaults of your enemy is heavily discounted by the fact that the enemy is equally immune from yours. In other words, you "get no forrarder" with a trench; and the one thing which we are all anxious to do out here is to bring this war to a speedy and gory conclusion, and get home to hot baths and regular meals.

So a few days ago we were not at all surprised to be informed, officially, that trench life is to be definitely abandoned, and Hun-hustling to begin in earnest.

(To be just, this decision was made months ago: the difficulty was to put it into execution. The winter weather was dreadful. The enemy were many and we were few. In Germany, the devil's forge at Essen was roaring night and day: in Great Britain Trades Union bosses were carefully adjusting the respective claims of patriotism and personal dignity before taking their coats off. So we cannot lay our want of progress to the charge of that dogged band of Greathearts which has been holding on, and holding on, and holding on — while the people at home were making up for lost time — ever since the barbarian was hurled back from the Marne to the Aisne and confined behind his earthen barrier. We shall win this war one day, and most of the credit will go, as usual, to those who are in at the finish. But — when we assign the glory and the praise, let us not forget those who stood up to the first rush. The new armies which are pouring across the Channel this month will bring us victory in the end. Let us bare our heads, then, in all reverence, to the memory of those battered, decimated, indomitable legions which saved us from utter extinction at the beginning.)

The situation appears to be that if we get through — and no one seems to doubt that we shall: the difficulty lies in staying there when you have got through — we shall be committed at once to an endless campaign of village-fighting. This country is as flat as Cambridgeshire. Every yard of it is under cultivation. The landscape is dotted with farm-steadings. There is a group of cottages or an *estaminet* at every cross-roads. When our great invading line sweeps forward, each one of these buildings will be held by the enemy, and must be captured, house by house, room by room, and used as a base for another rush.

And how is this to be done?

Well, it will be no military secret by the time these lines appear. It is no secret now. The answer to the conundrum is — Bombs!

Today, out here, bombs are absolutely *dernier cri*. We talk of nothing else. We speak about rifles and bayonets as if they were so many bows and arrows. It is true that the modern Lee-Enfield and Mauser claim to be the most precise and deadly weapons of destruction ever devised. But they were intended for proper, gentlemanly warfare, with the opposing sides set out in straight lines a convenient distance apart. In the hand-to-hand butchery which calls itself war today, the rifle is rapidly becoming *démodé*. For long ranges you require machine-guns; for short, bombs and hand-grenades. Can you empty a cottage by firing a single rifle-shot in at the door? Can you exterminate twenty Germans in a fortified back parlour by a single thrust with a bayonet? Never! But you can do both these things with a jam-tin stuffed with dynamite and scrap-iron.

So the bomb has come to its own, and has brought with it certain changes — tactical, organic, and domestic. To take the last first, the bomb-officer, hitherto a despised underling, popularly (but maliciously) reputed to have been appointed to his present post through inability to handle a platoon, has suddenly attained a position of dazzling eminence. From being a mere super, he has become a star. In fact, he threatens to dispute the pre-eminence of that other regimental parvenu, the Machine-Gun Officer. He is now the confidant of Colonels, and consorts upon terms of easy familiarity with Brigade Majors. He holds himself coldly aloof from the rest of us, brooding over the greatness of his responsibilities; and when he speaks, it is to refer darkly to "detonators", and "primers", and "time-fuses". And we, who once addressed him derisively as "Anarchist", crowd round him and hang upon his lips.

The reason is that in future it is to be a case of — "For every man, a bomb or two"; and it is incumbent upon us, if we desire to prevent these infernal machines from exploding while yet in our custody, to attain the necessary details as to their construction and tender spots by the humiliating process of conciliating the Bomb Officer.

So far as we have mastered the mysteries of the craft, there appear to be four types of bomb in store for us — or rather, for Brother Boche. They are:

(1) The hair-brush.
(2) The cricket-ball.
(3) The policeman's truncheon.
(4) The jam-tin.

The hair-brush is very like the ordinary hair-brush, except that the bristles are replaced by a solid block of high-explosive. The policeman's truncheon has gay streamers of tape tied to its tail, to ensure that it falls to the ground nose downwards. Both these bombs explode on impact, and it is unadvisable to knock them against anything — say the back of the trench — when throwing them. The cricket-ball works by a time-fuse. Its manipulation is simplicity itself. The removal of a certain pin releases a spring which lights an internal fuse, timed to explode the bomb in five seconds. You take the bomb in your right hand, remove the pin, and cast the thing madly from you. The jam-tin variety appeals more particularly to the sportsman, as the element of chance enters largely into its successful use. It is timed to explode about ten seconds after the lighting of the fuse. It is therefore unwise to throw it too soon, as there will be ample time for your opponent to pick it up and throw it back. On the other hand, it is unwise to hold on too long, as the fuse is uncertain in its action, and is given to short cuts.

Such is the tactical revolution promised by the advent of the bomb and other new engines of war. As for its effect upon regimental and company organisation, listen to the plaintive voice of Major Kemp:

"I was once — only a few months ago — commander of a company of two hundred and fifty disciplined soldiers. I still nominally command that company, but they have developed into a heterogeneous mob of specialists. If I detail one of my subalterns to do a job of work, he reminds me that he is a bomb-expert, or a professor of sandbagging, or director of the knuckle-duster section, or Lord High Thrower of Stink-pots, and as such has no time to play about with such a common thing as a platoon. As for the men, they simply laugh in the sergeant-major's face. They are 'experts', if you please, and are struck off all fatigues and company duty! It was bad enough when Ayling pinched fourteen of my best men for his filthy machine-guns; now, the company has practically degenerated into an academy of variety artists. The only occasion upon which I ever see them all together is pay-day!"

Meanwhile, the word has just gone forth, quietly and without fuss, that we are to uproot ourselves from our present billets, and be ready to move at 5 A.M. tomorrow morning.

Is this the Big Push at last?

*   *   *   *

We have been waiting for the best part of two days and nights listening to the thunder of the big guns, but as yet we have received no invitation to "butt in".

"Plenty of time yet," explains Captain Blaikie to his subalterns, in reply to Bobby Little's expressions of impatience. "It's this way. We start by 'isolating' a section of the enemy's line, and pound it with artillery for about forty-eight hours. Then the guns knock off, and the people in front rush the German first-line trenches. After that they push on to their second and third lines; and if they can capture and *hold them* — well, that's where the fun comes in. We go for all we are worth through the gaps the others have made, and carry on the big push, and keep the Boches on the run until they drop in their tracks! That's the situation. If we are called up tonight or tomorrow, it will mean that things are going well. If not, it means that the attack has failed — or, very likely, has succeeded, but it has been found impossible to secure the position — and a lot of good chaps have been scuppered, all for nothing."

*　　*　　*　　*

Next morning has arrived, and with it the news that our services will not be required. The attack, it appears, was duly launched, and succeeded beyond all expectations. The German line was broken, and report says that four Divisions poured through the gap. They captured the second-line trenches, then the third, and penetrated far into the enemy's rear.

Then — from their front and flanks, artillery and machine-guns open fire upon them. They were terribly exposed; possibly they had been lured into a trap. At any rate, the process of "isolation" had not been carried far enough. One thing, and only one thing, could have saved them from destruction and their enterprise from disaster — the support of big guns, and big guns, and more big guns. These could have silenced the hostile tornado of shrapnel and bullets, and the position could have been made good.

But — apparently the supply of big-gun ammunition is not quite so copious as it might be. We have only been at war ten months, and people at home are still a little dazed with the novelty of their situation. Out here, we are reasonable men, and we realise that it requires some time to devise a system for supplying munitions which shall hurt the feelings of no pacifist, which shall interfere with no man's holiday or glass of beer, which shall insult no honest toiler by compelling him to work side by side with those who are not of his industrial tabernacle, and which shall imperil no statesman's seat in Parliament. Things will be all right presently.

Meanwhile, the attacking party fell back whence they came — but no longer four full Divisions.

CHAPTER EIGHTEEN

THE FRONT OF THE FRONT

WE TOOK OVER these trenches a few days ago; and as the Germans are barely two hundred yards away, this chapter seems to justify its title.

For reasons foreshadowed, we find that we are committed to an indefinite period of trench life, like every one else.

Certainly we are starting at the bottom of the ladder. These trenches are badly sited, badly constructed, difficult of access from the rear, and swarming with large, fat, unpleasant flies, of the bluebottle variety. They go to sleep, chiefly upon the ceiling of one's dug-out, during the short hours of darkness, but for twenty hours out of twenty-four they are very busy indeed. They divide their attentions between stray carrion — there is a good deal hereabout — and our rations. If you sit still for five minutes they also settle upon *you*, like pins in a pin-cushion. Then, when face, hands, and knees can endure no more, and the inevitable convulsive wriggle occurs, they rise in a vociferous swarm, only to settle again when the victim becomes quiescent. To these, high-explosives are a welcome relief.

The trenches themselves are no garden city, like those at Armentières. They were sited and dug in the dark, not many weeks ago, to secure two hundred yards of French territory recovered from the Boche by bomb and bayonet. (The captured trench lies behind us now, and serves as our second line.) They are muddy — you come to water at three feet — and at one end, owing to their concave formation, are open to enfilade. The parapet in many places is too low. If you make it higher with sandbags you offer the enemy a comfortable target: if you deepen the trench you turn it into a running stream. Therefore long-legged subalterns crawl painfully past these danger-spots on all-fours, envying Little Tich.

Then there is Zacchæus. We call him by this name because he lives up a tree. There is a row of pollarded willows standing parallel to our front, a hundred and fifty yards away. Up, or in, one of these lives Zacchæus. We have never seen him, but we know he is there; because if you look over the top of the parapet he shoots you through the head. We do not even know which of the trees he lives in. There are nine of them, and every morning we comb them out, one by one, with a machine-gun. But all in vain. Zacchæus merely crawls away into the standing corn behind his trees, and waits till we have finished. Then he comes back and tries to shoot the machine-gun officer. He has not succeeded yet, but he sticks to his task with gentle persistence. He is evidently of a persevering rather than vindictive disposition.

Then there is Unter den Linden. This celebrated thoroughfare is an old communication trench. It runs, half-ruined, from the old German trench in our rear, right through our own front line, to the present German trenches. It constitutes such a bogey as the Channel Tunnel scheme once was: each side sits jealously at its own end, anticipating hostile enterprises from the other. It is also the residence of "Minnie". But we will return to Minnie later.

The artillery of both sides, too, contributes its mite. There is a dull roar far in the rear of the German trenches, followed by a whirring squeak overhead. Then comes an earth-shaking crash a mile behind us. We whip round, and there, in the failing evening light, against the sunset, there springs up the silhouette of a mighty tree in full foliage. Presently the silhouette disperses, drifts away, and —

"The coals is hame, right enough!" comments Private Tosh.

Instantly our guns reply, and we become the humble spectators of an artillery duel. Of course, if the enemy gets tired of "searching" the countryside for our guns and takes to "searching" our trenches instead, we lose all interest in the proceedings, and retire to our dug-outs, hoping that no direct hits will come our way.

But guns are notoriously erratic in their time-tables, and fickle in their attentions. It is upon Zacchæus and Unter den Linden — including Minnie — that we mainly rely for excitement.

As already recorded, we took over these trenches a few days ago, in the small hours of the morning. In the ordinary course of events, relieving parties are usually able to march up under cover of darkness to the reserve trench, half a mile in rear of the firing line, and so proceed to their appointed place. But on this occasion the German artillery happened to be "distributing coal" among the billets behind. This made it necessary to approach our new home by tortuous ways, and to take to subterranean courses at a very early stage of the journey. For more than two hours we toiled along a trench just wide enough to permit a man to wear his equipment, sometimes bent double to avoid the bullets of snipers, sometimes knee-deep in glutinous mud.

Ayling, leading a machine-gun section who were burdened with their weapons and seven thousand rounds of ammunition, mopped his streaming brow and inquired of his guide how much farther there was to go.

"Abart two miles, sir," replied the youth with gloomy satisfaction. He was a private of the Cockney regiment whom we were relieving; and after the manner of his kind, would infinitely have preferred to conduct us down half a mile of a shell-swept road, leading straight to the heart of things, than waste time upon an uninteresting but safe *détour*.

At this Ayling's Number One, who was carrying a machine-gun tripod weighing forty-eight pounds, said something — something distressingly audible — and groaned deeply.

"If we'd come the way I wanted," continued the guide, much pleased with the effect of his words upon his audience, "we'd a' been there be now. But the Adjutant, 'e says to me —"

"If we had come the way you wanted," interrupted Ayling brutally, "we should probably have been in Kingdom Come by now. Hurry up!" Ayling, in common with the rest of those present, was not in the best of tempers, and the loquacity of the guide had been jarring upon him for some time.

The Cockney private, with the air of a deeply-wronged man, sulkily led on, followed by the dolorous procession. Another ten minutes' laboured progress brought them to a place where several ways met.

"This is the beginning of the reserve trenches, sir," announced the guide. "If we'd come the way I —"

"Lead on!" said Ayling, and his perspiring followers murmured threatening applause.

The guide, now in his own territory, selected the muddiest opening and plunged down it. For two hundred yards or so he continued serenely upon his way, with the air of one exhibiting the Metropolis to a party of country cousins. He passed numerous turnings. Then, once or twice, he paused irresolutely; then moved on. Finally he halted, and proceeded to climb out of the trench.

"What are you doing?" demanded Ayling suspiciously.

"We got to cut across the open 'ere, sir," said the youth glibly. "Trench don't go no farther. Keep as low as you can."

With resigned grunts the weary pilgrims hoisted themselves and their numerous burdens out of their slimy thoroughfare, and followed their conductor through the long grass in single file, feeling painfully conspicuous against the whitening sky. Presently they discovered, and descended into, another trench — all but the man with the tripod, who descended into it before he discovered it — and proceeded upon their dolorous way. Once more the guide, who had been refreshingly but ominously silent for some time, paused irresolutely.

"Look here, my man," said Ayling, "do you, or do you not, know where you are?"

The paragon replied hesitatingly —

"Well, sir, if we'd come by the way I —"

Ayling took a deep breath, and though conscious of the presence of formidable competitors, was about to make the best of an officer's vocabulary, when a kilted figure loomed out of the darkness.

"Hallo! Who are you?" inquired Ayling.

"This iss the Camerons' trenches, sirr," replied a polite West Highland voice. "What trenches wass you seeking?"

Ayling told him.

"They are behind you, sirr."

"I was just goin' to say, sir," chanted the guide, making one last effort to redeem his prestige, "as 'ow —"

"Party," commanded Ayling, "about turn!"

Having received details of the route from the friendly Cameron, he scrambled out of the trench and crawled along to what was now the head of the procession. A plaintive voice followed him.

"Beg pardon, sir, where shall *I* go now?"

Ayling answered the question explicitly, and moved off, feeling much better. The late conductor of the party trailed disconsolately in the rear.

"I should like to know wot I'm 'ere for," he murmered indignantly.

He got his answer, like a lightning-flash.

"For tae carry *this*," said the man with the tripod, turning round. "Here, caatch!"

*   *   *   *

The day's work in trenches begins about nine o'clock the night before. Darkness having fallen, various parties steal out into the No-man's-land beyond the parapet. There are numerous things to be done. The barbed wire has been broken up by shrapnel, and must be repaired. The whole position in front of the wire must be patrolled, to prevent the enemy from creeping forward in the dark. The corn has grown to an uncomfortable height in places, so a fatigue party is told off to cut it — surely the strangest species of harvesting that the annals of agriculture can record. On the left front the muffled clinking of picks and shovels announces that a "sap" is in course of construction: those incorrigible night-birds, the Royal Engineers, are making it for the machine-gunners, who in the fulness of time will convey their voluble weapon to its forward extremity, and "loose off a belt or two" in the direction of a rather dangerous hollow midway between the trenches, from which of late mysterious sounds of digging and guttural talking have been detected by the officer who lies in the listening-post, in front of our barbed-wire entanglement, drawing secrets from the bowels of the earth by means of a microphone.

Behind the firing trench even greater activity prevails. Damage done to the parapet by shell fire is being repaired. Positions and emplacements are being constantly improved, communication trenches widened or made more secure. Down these trenches fatigue parties are filing, to draw rations and water and ammunition from the limbered waggons which are waiting in the shadow of a wood, perhaps a mile back. It is at this hour, too, that the wounded, who have been lying pathetically cheerful and patient in the dressing station in the reserve trench, are smuggled to the Field Ambulance — probably to find themselves safe in a London hospital within twenty-four hours. Lastly, under the kindly cloak of night, we bury our dead.

Meanwhile, within various stifling dug-outs, in the firing trench or support trench, overheated company commanders are dictating reports or filling in returns. (Even now the Round Game Department is not entirely shaken off.) There is the casualty return, and a report of the doings of the enemy, and another report of one's own doings, and a report on the direction of the wind, and so on. Then there are various indents to fill up — scrawled on a wobbly writing-block with a blunt indelible pencil by the light of a guttering candle — for ammunition, and sandbags, and revetting material.

All this literature has to be sent to Battalion Headquarters by one A.M., either by orderly or telephone. There it is collated and condensed, and forwarded to the Brigade, which submits it to the same process and sends it on, to be served up piping hot and easily digestible at the breakfast-table of the Division, five miles away, at eight o'clock.

You must not imagine, however, that all this night-work is performed in gross darkness. On the contrary. There is abundance of illumination; and by a pretty thought, each side illuminates the other. We perform our nocturnal tasks, in front of and behind the firing trench, amid a perfect hail of star-shells and magnesium lights, topped up at times by a searchlight — all supplied by our obliging friend the Hun. We, on our part, do our best to return these graceful compliments.

The curious and uncanny part of it all is that there is no firing. During these brief hours there exists an informal truce, founded on the principle of live and let live. It would be an easy business to wipe out that working party, over there by the barbed wire, with a machine-gun. It would be child's play to shell the road behind the enemy's trenches, crowded as it must be with ration-waggons and water-carts, into a blood-stained wilderness. But so long as each side confines itself to purely defensive and recuperative work, there is little or no interference. That slave of duty, Zacchæus, keeps on pegging away; and occasionally, if a hostile patrol shows itself too boldly, there is a little exuberance from a machine-gun; but on the whole there is silence. After all, if you prevent your enemy from drawing his rations, his remedy is simple: he will prevent you from drawing yours. Then both parties will have to fight on empty stomachs, and neither of them, tactically, will be a penny the better. So, unless some elaborate scheme of attack is brewing, the early hours of the night are comparatively peaceful. But what is that sudden disturbance in the front-line trench? A British rifle rings out, then another, and another, until there is an agitated fusilade from end to end of the section. Instantly the sleepless host across the way replies, and for three minutes or so a hurricane rages. The working parties out in front lie flat on their faces, cursing patiently. Suddenly the storm dies away, and perfect silence reigns once more. It was a false alarm. Some watchman, deceived by the whispers of the night breeze, or merely a prey to nerves, has discerned a phantom army approaching through the gloom, and has opened fire thereon. This often occurs when troops are new to trench-work.

It is during these hours, too, that regiments relieve one another in the trenches. The outgoing regiment cannot leave its post until the incoming regiment has "taken over". Consequently you have, for a brief space, two thousand troops packed into a trench calculated to hold one thousand. Then it is that strong men swear themselves faint, and the Rugby football player has reason to be thankful for his previous training in the art of "getting through the scrum". However perfect your organisation may be, congestion is bound to occur here and there; and it is no little consolation to us to feel, as we surge and sway in the darkness, that over there in the German lines a Saxon and a Prussian private, irretrievably jammed together in a narrow communication trench, are consigning one another to perdition in just the same husky whisper as that employed by Private Mucklewame and his "opposite number" in the regiment which has come to relieve him.

These "reliefs" take place very four or five nights. There was a time, not so long ago, when a regiment was relieved, not when it was weary, but when another regiment could be found to replace it. Our own first battalion once remained in the trenches, unrelieved and only securing its supplies with difficulty, for five weeks and three days. During all that time they were subject to most pressing attentions on the part of the Boches, but they never lost a yard of trench. They received word from Headquarters that to detach another regiment for their relief would seriously weaken other and most important dispositions. The Commander-In-Chief would therefore be greatly obliged if they could hold on. So they held on.

At last they came out, and staggered back to billets. Their old quarters, naturally, had long been appropriated by other troops, and the officers had some difficulty in recovering their kits.

"I don't mind being kept in trenches for several

weeks," remarked their commander to the staff officer who received him when he reported, "and I can put up with losing my sleeping-bag; but I do object to having my last box of cigars looted by the blackguards who took over our billets!"

The staff officer expressed sympathy, and the subject dropped. But not many days later, while the battalion were still resting, their commander was roused in the middle of the night from the profound slumber which only the experience of many nights of anxious vigil can induce, by the ominous message —

"An orderly to see you, from General Headquarters, sir!"

The colonel rolled stoically out of bed, and commanded that the orderly should be brought before him.

The man entered, carrying, not a despatch, but a package, which he proffered with a salute.

"With the Commander-in-Chief's compliments, sir!" he announced.

The package was a box of cigars!

But that was before the days of "K(1)".

But the night is wearing on. It is half-past one — time to knock off work. Tired men, returning from ration-drawing or sap-digging, throw themselves down and fall dead asleep in a moment. Only the sentries, with their elbows on the parapet, maintain their sleepless watch. From behind the enemy's lines comes a deep boom — then another. The big guns are waking up again, and have decided to commence their day's work by speeding our empty ration-waggons upon their homeward way. Let them! So long as they refrain from practising direct hits on our front-line parapet, and disturbing our brief and hardly-earned repose, they may fire where they please. The ration train is well able to look after itself.

"A whiff o' shrapnel will dae nae harrm to thae

strawberry-jam pinchers!" observes Private Tosh bitterly, rolling into his dug-out. By this opprobrious term he designates that distinguished body of men, the Army Service Corps. A prolonged diet of plum-and-apple jam has implanted in the breasts of the men in the trenches certain dark and unworthy suspicions concerning the entire altruism of those responsible for the distribution of the Army's rations.

It is close on daybreak, and the customary whispered order runs down the stertorous trench —

"Stand to arms!"

Straightway the parapets are lined with armed men; the waterproof sheets which have been protecting the machine-guns from the dews of night are cast off; and we stand straining our eyes into the whitening darkness.

This is the favourite hour of attack. At any moment the guns may open fire upon our parapet, or a solid wall of grey-clad figures rise from that strip of corn-land less than a hundred yards away, and descend upon us. Well, we are ready for them. Just by way of signalising the fact, there goes out a ragged volley of rifle fire, and a machine-gun rips off half a dozen bursts into the standing corn. But apparently there is nothing doing this morning. The day grows brighter, but there is no movement upon the part of Brother Boche.

But — what is that light haze hanging over the enemy's trenches? It is slight, almost impalpable, but it appears to be drifting towards us. Can it be —?

Next moment every man is hurriedly pulling his gas helmet over his head, while Lieutenant Waddell beats a frenzied tocsin upon the instrument provided for the purpose — to wit, an empty eighteen-pounder shell, which, suspended from a bayonet stuck into the parados (or back wall) of the trench, makes a most efficient alarm-gong. The sound is repeated all along the trench, and in two minutes every man is in his place, cowled like a member of the Holy Inquisition, glaring through an eye-piece of mica, and firing madly into the approaching wall of vapour.

But the wall approaches very slowly — in fact, it almost stands still — and finally, as the rising sun disentangles itself from a pink horizon and climbs into the sky, it begins to disappear. In half an hour nothing is left, and we take off our helmets, sniffing the morning air dubiously. But all we smell is the old mixture — corpses and chloride of lime.

The incident, however, was duly recorded by Major Kemp in his report of the day's events, as follows:

4.7 A.M. — Gas alarm, false. Due either to morning mist, or the fact that enemy found breeze insufficient, and discontinued their attempt.

"Still, I'm not sure," he continued, slapping his bald head with a bandana handkerchief, "that a whiff of chlorine or bromine wouldn't do these trenches a considerable amount of good. It would tone down some of the deceased a bit, and wipe out these infernal flies. Waddell, if I give you a shilling, will you take it over to the German trenches and ask them to drop it into the meter?"

"I do not think, sir," replied the literal Waddell, "that an English shilling would fit a German meter. Probably a mark would be required, and I have only a franc. Besides, sir, do you think that —"

"Surgical operation at seven-thirty, sharp!" intimated the major to the medical officer, who entered the dug-out at that moment. "For our friend here" — indicating the bewildered Waddell. "Sydney Smith's prescription! Now, what about breakfast?"

About nine o'clock the enemy indulges in what is usually described, most disrespectfully, as "a little morning hate" — in other words, a bombardment.

Beginning with a *hors d'œuvre* of shrapnel along the reserve trench — much to the discomfort of Headquarters, who are shaving — he proceeds to "search" a tract of woodland in our immediate rear, his quarry being a battery of motor machine-guns, which has wisely decamped some hours previously. Then, after scientifically "traversing" our second line, which has rashly advertised its position and range by cooking its breakfast over a smoky fire, he brings the display to a superfluous conclusion by dropping six "Black Marias" into the deserted ruins of a village not far behind us. After that comes silence; and we are able, in our hot, baking trenches, assisted by clouds of bluebottles, to get on with the day's work.

This consists almost entirely in digging. As already stated, these are bad trenches. The parapet is none too strong — at one point it has been knocked down for three days running — the communication trenches are few and narrow, and there are not nearly enough dugouts. Yesterday three men were wounded; and owing to the impossibility of carrying a stretcher along certain parts of the trench, they had to be conveyed to the rear in their ground-sheets — bumped against projections, bent round sharp corners, and sometimes lifted, perforce, bodily into view of the enemy. So every man toils with a will, knowing full well that in a few hours' time he may prove to have been his own benefactor. Only the sentries remain at the parapets. They no longer expose themselves, as at night, but take advantage of the laws of optical reflection, as exemplified by the trench periscope. (This, in spite of its grand title, is nothing but a tiny mirror clipped on to a bayonet.)

At half-past twelve comes dinner — bully-beef, with biscuit and jam — after which each tired man, coiling himself up in the trench, or crawling underground, according to the accommodation at his disposal, drops off into instant and heavy slumber. The hours from two till five in the afternoon are usually the most uneventful of the twenty-four, and are therefore devoted to hardly-earned repose.

But there is to be little peace this afternoon. About half-past three, Bobby Little, immersed in pleasant dreams — dreams of cool shades and dainty companionship — is brought suddenly to the surface of things by —

"Whoo-oo-*oo*-oo-UMP!"

— followed by a heavy thud upon the roof of his dug-out. Earth and small stones descend in a shower upon him.

"Dirty dogs!" he comments, looking at his watch. Then he puts his head out of the dug-out.

"Lie close, you men!" he cries. "There's more of this coming. Any casualties?"

The answer to the question is obscured by another burst of shrapnel, which explodes a few yards short of the parapet, and showers bullets and fragments of shell into the trench. A third and a fourth follow. Then comes a pause. A message is passed down for the stretcher-bearers. Things are growing serious. Five minutes later Bobby, having despatched his wounded to the dressing station, proceeds with all haste to Captain Blaikie's dug-out.

"How many, Bobby?"

"Six wounded. Two of them won't last as far as the rear, I'm afraid, sir."

Captain Blaikie looks grave.

"Better ring up the Gunners, I think. Where are the shells coming from?"

"That wood on our left front, I think."

"That's P 27. Telephone orderly, there?"

A figure appears in the doorway.

"Yes, sirr."

"Ring up Major Cavanagh, and say that H 21 is being shelled from P 27. Retaliate!"

193

"Verra good, sirr."

The telephone orderly disappears, to return in five minutes.

"Major Cavanagh's compliments, sirr, and he is coming up himself for tae observe from the firing trench."

"Good egg!" observes Captain Blaikie. "Now we shall see some shooting, Bobby!"

Presently the Gunner major arrives, accompanied by an orderly, who pays out wire as he goes. The major adjusts his periscope, while the orderly thrusts a metal peg into the ground and fits a telephone receiver to his head.

"Number one gun!" chants the major, peering into his periscope; "three-five-one-nothing — lyddite — fourth charge!"

These mystic observations are repeated into the telephone by the Cockney orderly, in a confidential undertone.

"Report when ready!" continues the major.

"Report when ready!" echoes the orderly.

Then — "Number one gun ready, sir!"

"Fire!"

"Fire!" Then, politely — "Number one has fired, sir."

The major stiffens to his periscope, and Bobby Little, deeply interested, wonders what has become of the report of the gun. He forgets that sound does not travel much faster than a thousand feet a second, and that the guns are a mile and a half back. Presently, however, there is a distant boom. Almost simultaneously the lyddite shell passes overhead with a scream. Bobby, having no periscope, cannot see the actual result of the shot, though he tempts Providence (and Zacchæus) by peering over the top of the parapet.

"Number one, two-nothing minutes more right," commands the major. "Same range and charge."

Once more the orderly goes through his ritual, and

presently another shell screams overhead.

Again the major observes the result.

"Repeat!" he says. "Nothing—five seconds more right."

This time he is satisfied.

"Parallel lines on number one," he commands crisply. "One round battery fire — twenty seconds!"

For the last time the order is passed down the wire, and the major hands his periscope to the ever-grateful Bobby, who has hardly got his eyes to the glass when the round of battery fire commences. One — two — three — four — the avenging shells go shrieking on their way, at intervals of twenty seconds. There are four muffled thuds, and four great columns of earth and *débris* spring up before the wood. Answer comes there none. The offending battery has prudently effaced itself.

"Cease fire!" says the major, "and register!" Then he turns to Captain Blaikie.

"That'll settle them for a bit," he observes. "By the way, had any more trouble with Minnie?"

"We had Hades from her yesterday," replies Blaikie, in answer to this extremely personal question. "She started at a quarter-past five in the morning, and went on till about ten."

(Perhaps, at this point, it would be as well to introduce Minnie a little more formally. She is the most unpleasant of her sex, and her full name is *Minenwerfer,* or German trench-mortar. She resides, spasmodically, in Unter den Linden. Her extreme range is about two hundred yards, so she confines her attentions to front-line trenches. Her *modus operandi* is to discharge a large cylindrical bomb into the air. The bomb, which is about fifteen inches long and some eight inches in diameter, describes a leisurely parabola, performing grotesque somersaults on the way, and finally falls with a soft thud into the trench, or against the parapet.

There, after an interval of ten seconds, Minnie's off-spring explodes; and as she contains about thirty pounds of dynamite, no dug-out or parapet can stand against her.)

"Did she do much damage?" inquires the Gunner.

"Killed two men and buried another. They were in a dug-out."

The Gunner shakes his head.

"No good taking cover against Minnie," he says. "The only way is to come out into the open trench, and dodge her."

"So we found," replies Blaikie. "But they pulled our legs badly the first time. They started off with three 'whizz-bangs'" — a whizz-bang is a particularly offensive form of shell which bursts two or three times over, like a Chinese cracker — "so we all took cover and lay low. The consequence was that Minnie was able to send her little contribution along unobserved. The filthy thing fell short of the trench, and exploded just as we were all getting up again. It smashed up three or four yards of parapet, and scuppered the three poor chaps I mentioned."

"Have you located her?"

"Yes. Just behind that stunted willow, on our left front. I fancy they bring her along there to do her bit, and then trot her back to the billets, out of harm's way. She is their two o'clock turn — two A.M. and two P.M."

"Two o'clock turn — h'm!" says the Gunner major meditatively. "What about our chipping in with a one-fifty-five turn — half a dozen H.E. shells into Minnie's dressing-room — eh? I must think this over."

"Do!" said Blaikie cordially. "Minnie is Willie's Worst Werfer, and the sooner she is put out of action the better for all of us. Today, for some reason, she failed to appear, but previous to that she has not failed for five mornings in succession to batter down the same bit of our parapet."

"Where's that?" asks the major, getting out a trench-map.

"P 7 — a most unhealthy spot. Minnie pushes it over about two every morning. The result is that we have to mount guard over the breach all day. We build everything up again at night, and Minnie sits there as good as gold, and never dreams of interfering. You can almost hear her cooing over us. Then, as I say, at two o'clock, just as the working party comes in and gets under cover, she lets slip one of her disgusting bombs, and undoes the work of about four hours. It was a joke at first, but we are getting fed up now. That's the worst of the Boche. He starts by being playful; but if not suppressed at once, he gets rough; and that, of course, spoils all the harmony of the proceedings. So I cordially commend your idea of the one-fifty-five turn, sir."

"I'll see what can be done," says the major. "I think the best plan would be a couple of hours' solid frightfulness, from every battery we can switch on. Tomorrow afternoon, perhaps, but I'll let you know. You'll have to clear out of this bit of trench altogether, as we shall shoot pretty low. So long!"

    *   *   *   *

It is six o'clock next evening, and peace reigns over our trench. This is the hour at which one usually shells aeroplanes — or rather, at which the Germans shell ours, for their own seldom venture out in broad daylight. But this evening, although two or three are up in the blue, buzzing inquisitively over the enemy's lines, their attendant escort of white shrapnel puffs is entirely lacking. Far away behind the German lines a house is burning fiercely.

"The Hun is a bit *piano* tonight," observes Captain Blaikie, attacking his tea.

"The Hun has been rather firmly handled this afternoon," replies Captain Wagstaffe. "I think he has had

197

an eye-opener. There are no flies on our Divisional Artillery."

Bobby Little heaved a contented sigh. For two hours that afternoon he had sat, half-deafened, while six-inch shells skimmed the parapet in both directions, a few feet above his head. The Gunner major had been as good as his word. Punctually at one-fifty-five Minnie's two o'clock turn had been anticipated by a round of high-explosive shells directed into her suspected place of residence. What the actual result had been nobody knew, but Minnie had made no attempt to raise her voice since. Thereafter the German front-line trenches had been "plastered" from end to end, while the trenches farther back were attended to with methodical thoroughness. The German guns had replied vigorously, but directing only a passing fire at the trenches, had devoted their efforts chiefly to the silencing of the British artillery. In this enterprise they had been remarkably unsuccessful.

"Any casualties?" asked Blaikie.

"None here," replied Wagstaffe. "There may be some back in the support trenches."

"We might telephone and inquire."

"No good at present. The wires are all cut to pieces. The signallers are repairing them now."

"*I* was nearly a casualty," confessed Bobby modestly.

"How?"

"That first shell of ours nearly knocked my head off! I was standing up at the time, and it rather took me by surprise. It just cleared the parados. In fact, it kicked a lot of gravel into the back of my neck."

"Most people get it in the neck here, sooner or later," remarked Captain Blaikie sententiously. "Personally, I don't much mind being killed, but I do bar being buried alive. That is why I dislike Minnie so." He rose, and stretched himself. "Heigho! I suppose it's about time we detailed patrols and working parties for tonight. What a lovely sky! A truly peaceful atmosphere — what! It gives one a sort of Sunday-evening feeling, somehow."

"May I suggest an explanation?" said Wagstaffe.

"By all means."

"It *is* Sunday evening!"

Captain Blaikie whistled gently, and said —

"By Jove, so it is." Then, after a pause: "This time last Sunday —"

Last Sunday had been an off-day — a day of cloudless summer beauty. Tired men had slept; tidy men had washed their clothes; restless men had wandered at ease about the countryside, careless of the guns which grumbled everlastingly a few miles away. There had been impromptu Church Parades for each denomination, in a corner of a wood which was part of the demesne of a shell-torn chateau.

It is a sadly transformed wood. The open space before the chateau, once a smooth expanse of tennis-lawn, is now a dusty picketing-ground for transport mules, destitute of a single blade of grass. The ornamental lake is full of broken bottles and empty jam-tins. The pagoda-like summer-house, so inevitable to French chateau gardens, is a quartermaster's store. Half the trees have been cut down for fuel. Still, the July sun streams very pleasantly through the remainder, and the Psalms of David float up from beneath their shade quite as sweetly as they usually do from the neighbourhood of the precentor's desk in the kirk at home — perhaps sweeter.

The wood itself is a *point d'appui*, or fortified post. One has to take precautions, even two or three miles behind the main firing line. A series of trenches zigzags in and out among the trees, and barbed wire is interlaced with the undergrowth. In the farthermost corner lies an improvised cemetery. Some of the inscriptions on the little wooden crosses are only three days old.

Merely to read a few of these touches the imagination and stirs the blood. Here you may see the names of English Tommies and Highland Jocks, side by side with their Canadian kith and kin. A little apart lie more graves, surmounted by epitaphs written in strange characters, such as few white men can read. These are the Indian troops. There they lie, side by side — the mute wastage of war, but a living testimony, even in their last sleep, to the breadth and unity of the British Empire. The great machine-made Empire of Germany can show no such graves: when her soldiers die, they sleep alone.

The Church of England service had come last of all. Late in the afternoon a youthful and red-faced chaplain had arrived on a bicycle, to find a party of officers and men lying in the shade of a broad oak waiting for him. (They were a small party: naturally, the great majority of the regiment are what the identity-discs call "Pres" or "R.C.")

"Sorry to be late, sir," he said to the senior officer, saluting. "This is my sixth sh — service today, and I have come seven miles for it."

He mopped his brow cheerfully; and having produced innumerable hymn-books from a saddle-bag and set his congregation in array, read them the service, in a particularly pleasing and well-modulated voice. After that he preached a modest and manly little sermon, containing references which carried Bobby Little, for one, back across the Channel to other scenes and other company. After the sermon came a hymn, sung with great vigour. Tommy loves singing hymns — when he happens to know and like the tune.

"I know you chaps like hymns," said the padre, when they had finished. "Let's have another before you go. What do you want?"

A most unlikely-looking person suggested *Abide with Me*. When it was over, and the party, standing as rigid as their own rifles, had sung *God Save the King*, the preacher announced, awkwardly — almost apologetically —

"If any of you would like to — er — communicate, I shall be very glad. May not have another opportunity for some time, you know. I think over there" — he indicated a quiet corner of the wood, not far from the little cemetery — "would be a good place."

He pronounced the benediction, and then, after further recurrence to his saddle-bag, retired to his improvised sanctuary. Here, with a ration-box for altar, and strands of barbed wire for choir-stalls, he made his simple preparations.

Half a dozen of the men, and all the officers, followed him. That was just a week ago.

Captain Wagstaffe broke the silence at last.

"It's a rotten business, war," he said pensively — "when you come to think of it. Hallo, there goes the first star-shell! Come along, Bobby!"

Dusk had fallen. From the German trenches a thin luminous thread stole up into the darkening sky, leaned over, drooped, and burst into dazzling brilliance over the British parapet. Simultaneously a desultory rifle fire cracked down the lines. The night's work had begun.

CHAPTER NINETEEN

THE TRIVIAL ROUND

WE HAVE BEEN occupying trenches, off and on, for a matter of two months, and have settled down to an unexhilarating but salutary routine. Each dawn we "stand to arms", and peer morosely over the parapet, watching the grey grass turn slowly to green, while snipers' bullets buzz over our heads. Each forenoon we cleanse our dew-rusted weapons, and build up with sand-bags what the persevering Teuton has thrown down. Each afternoon we creep unostentatiously into subterranean burrows, while our respective gunners, from a safe position in the rear, indulge in what they humorously describe as "an artillery duel". The humour arises from the fact that they fire, not at one another, but at us. It is as if two big boys, having declared a vendetta, were to assuage their hatred and satisfy their honour by going out every afternoon and throwing stones at one another's little brothers. Each evening we go on sentry duty; or go out with patrols, or working parties, or ration parties. Our losses in killed and wounded are not heavy, but they are regular. We would not grudge the lives thus spent if only we could advance, even a little. But there is nothing doing. Sometimes a trench is rushed here, or recaptured there, but the net result is — stalemate.

The campaign upon which we find ourselves at present embarked offers few opportunities for brilliancy. One wonders how Napoleon would have handled it. His favourite device, we remember, was to dash rapidly about the chessboard, insert himself between two hostile armies, and defeat them severally. But how can you insert yourself between two armies when you are faced by only one army — an army stretching from Ostend to the Alps?

One of the first elements of successful strategy is surprise. In the old days, a general of genius could outflank his foe by a forced march, or lay some ingenious trap or ambush. But how can you outflank a foe who has no flanks? How can you lay an ambush for the modern Intelligence Department, with its aeroplane reconnaissance and telephonic nervous system? Do you mass half a million men at a chosen point in the enemy's line? Straightway the enemy knows all about it, and does likewise. Each morning General Headquarters of each side finds upon its breakfast-table a concise summary of the movements of all hostile troops, the disposition of railway rolling-stock — yea, even aeroplane photographs of it all. What could Napoleon himself have done under the circumstances? One is inclined to suspect that that volcanic megalomaniac would have perished of spontaneous combustion of the brain.

However, trench life has its alleviations. There is The Day's Work, for instance. Each of us has his own particular "stunt", in which he takes that personal and rather egotistical pride which only increasing proficiency can bestow.

The happiest — or at least, the busiest — people just now are the "Specialists". If you are engaged in ordinary Company work, your energies are limited to keeping watch, dodging shells, and improving trenches. But if you are what is invidiously termed an "employed" man, life is full of variety.

Do you observe that young officer sitting on a ration-box at his dug-out door, with his head tied up in a bandage? That is Second Lieutenant Lochgair, whom I hope to make better known to you in time. He is a chieftain of high renown in his own inaccessible but extensive fastness; but out here, where every man stands on his own legs, and not his grandfather's, he is known simply as "Othello". This is due to the fact that Major Kemp once likened him to the earnest young actor of tradition, who blacked himself all over to ensure proficiency in the playing of that part. For he is above all things an enthusiast in his profession. Last night he volunteered to go out and "listen" for a suspected mine some fifty yards from the German trenches. He set out as soon as darkness fell, taking with him a biscuit-tin full of water. A circular from Head-quarters — one of those circulars which no one but Othello would have treated with proper reverence — had suggested this device. The idea was that, since liquids convey sound better than air, the listener should place his tin of water on the ground, lie down beside it, immerse one ear therein, and so draw secrets from the earth. Othello failed to locate the mine, but kept his head in the biscuit-tin long enough to contract a severe attack of earache.

But he is not discouraged. At present he is meditat-ing a design for painting himself grass-green and climbing a tree — thence to take a comprehensive and unobserved survey of the enemy's dispositions. He will do it, too, if he gets a chance!

The machine-gunners, also, contrive to chase mon-otony by methods of their own. Listen to Ayling, con-cocting his diurnal scheme of frightfulness with a col-league. Unrolled upon his knee is a large-scale map.

"I think we might touch up those cross-roads tonight," he says, laying the point of his dividers upon a spot situated some hundreds of yards in rear of the German trenches. "I expect they'll have lots of transport there about ration-time — eh?"

"Sound scheme," assents his coadjutor, a blood-thirsty stripling named Ainslie. "Got the bearings?"

"Hand me that protractor. Seventy-one, nineteen, true. That comes to" — Ayling performs a mental calculation — "almost exactly eight-five, magnetic. We'll go out about nine, with two guns, to the corner of this dry ditch here — the range is two thousand five hundred, exactly" —

"Our lightning calculator!" murmurs his admiring colleague. "No elastic up the sleeve, or anything! All done by simple ledger-de-mang? Proceed!"

— "And loose off a belt or two. What say?"

"Application forwarded, and strongly recommended," announced Ainslie. He examined the map. "Cross-roads — eh? That means at least one estaminet. One estaminet, with Boches inside, complete! Think of our little bullets all popping in through the open door, five hundred a minute! Think of the rush to crawl under the counter! It might be a Headquarters? We might get Von Kluck or Rupy of Bavaria, splitting a half-litre together. We shall earn Military Crosses over this, my boy," concluded the imaginative youth. "Wow, wow!"

"The worst of indirect fire," mused the less gifted Ayling, "is that you never can tell whether you have hit your target or not. In fact, you can't even tell whether there was a target there to hit."

"Never mind; we'll chance it," replied Ainslie. "And if the Boche artillery suddenly wakes up and begins retaliating on the wrong spot with whizz-bangs — well, we shall know we've tickled up *somebody*, anyhow! Nine o'clock, you say?"

Here, again, is a bombing party, prepared to steal out under cover of night. They are in charge of one Simson, recently promoted to Captain, supported by that hoary fire-eater, Sergeant Carfrae. The party numbers seven all told, the only other member thereof with whom we are personally acquainted being Lance-Corporal McSnape, the ex-Boy Scout. Every man wears a broad canvas belt full of pockets: each pocket contains a bomb.

Simson briefly outlines the situation. Our fire-trench here runs round the angle of an orchard, which brings it uncomfortably close to the Germans. The Germans are quite as uncomfortable about the fact as we are — some of us are rather inclined to overlook this important feature of the case — and they have run a sap out towards the nearest point of the Orchard Trench (so our aeroplane observers report), in order to supervise our movements more closely.

"It may only be a listening-post," explains Simson to his bombers, "with one or two men in it. On the other hand, they may be collecting a party to rush us. There are some big shell-craters there, and they may be using one of them as a saphead. Anyhow, our orders are to go out tonight and see. If we find the sap, with any Germans in it, we are to bomb them out of it, and break up the sap as far as possible. Advance, and follow me."

The party steals out. The night is very still, and a young and inexperienced moon is making a somewhat premature appearance behind the Boche trenches. The ground is covered with weedy grass — disappointed hay — which makes silent progress a fairly simple matter. The bombers move forward in extended order searching for the saphead. Simson, in the centre, pauses occasionally to listen, and his well-drilled line pauses with him. Sergeant Carfrae calls stertorously upon the left. Out on the right is young McSnape, tingling.

They are half-way across now, and the moon is marking time behind a cloud.

Suddenly there steals to the ears of McSnape —

apparently from the recesses of the earth just in front of him — a deep hollow sound, the sound of men talking in some cavernous space. He stops dead, and signals to his companions to do likewise. Then he listens again. Yes, he can distinctly hear guttural voices, and an occasional *clink, clink*. The saphead has been reached, and digging operations are in progress.

A whispered order comes down the line that McSnape is to "investigate". He wriggles forward until his progress is arrested by a stunted bush. Very stealthily he rises to his knees and peers over. As he does so, a chance star-shell bursts squarely over him, and comes sizzling officiously down almost on to his back. His head drops like a stone into the bush, but not before the ghostly magnesium flare has shown him what he came out to see — a deep shell-crater. The crater is full of Germans. They look like grey beetles in a trap, and are busy with pick and shovel, apparently "improving" the crater and connecting it with their own fire-trenches. They have no sentry out. *Dormitat Homerus.*

McSnape worms his way back, and reports. Then, in accordance with an oft-rehearsed scheme, the bombing party forms itself into an arc of a circle at a radius of some twenty yards from the stunted bush. (Not the least of the arts of bomb-throwing is to keep out of the range of your own bombs.) Every man's hand steals to his pocketed belt. Next moment Simson flings the first bomb. It flies fairly into the middle of the crater.

Half a dozen more go swirling after it. There is a shattering roar; a cloud of smoke; a muffled rush of feet; silence; some groans. Almost simultaneously the German trenches are in an uproar. A dozen star-shells leap to the sky; there is a hurried outburst of rifle fire; a machine-gun begins to patter out a stuttering malediction.

Meanwhile our friends, who have exhibited no pedantic anxiety to remain and behold the result of their labours, are lying upon their stomachs in a convenient fold in the ground, waiting patiently until such time as it shall be feasible to complete their homeward journey.

Half an hour later they do so, and roll one by one over the parapet into the trench. Casualties are slight. Private Nimmo has a bullet-wound in the calf of his leg; and Sergeant Carfrae, whom Nature does not permit to lie as flat as the others, will require some repairs to the pleats of his kilt.

"All present?" inquires Simson.

It is discovered that McSnape has not returned. Anxious eyes peer over the parapet. The moon is stronger now, but it is barely possible to distinguish objects clearly for more than a few yards.

A star-shell bursts, and heads sink below the parapet. A German bullet passes overhead, with a sound exactly like the crack of a whip. Silence and comparative darkness return. The heads go up again.

"I'll give him five minutes more, and then go and look for him," says Simson. "Hallo!"

A small bush, growing just outside the barbed wire, rises suddenly to its feet; and, picking its way with incredible skill through the nearest opening, runs at full speed for the parapet. Next moment it tumbles over into the trench.

Willing hands extracted McSnape from his arboreal envelope — he could probably have got home quite well without it, but once a Boy Scout, always a Boy Scout — and he made his report.

"I went back to have a look-see into the crater, sirr."

"Well?"

"It's fair blown in, sirr, and a good piece of the sap too. I tried could I find a prisoner to bring in" — our Colonel has promised a reward of fifty francs to the man who can round up a whole live Boche — "but there were nane. They had got their wounded away, I doubt."

"Never mind," says Simson. "Sergeant, see these men get some sleep now. Stand-to at two-thirty, as usual. I must go and pitch in a report, and I shall say you all did splendidly. Good night!"

This morning the official Intelligence Summary of our Division — published daily and known to the unregenerate as "Comic Cuts" — announced, with solemn relish, among other items of news:

Last night a small party bombed a suspected saphead at — here followed the exact bearings of the crater on the large-scale map. *Loud groans were heard, so it is probable that the bombs took effect.*

For the moment, life has nothing more to offer to our seven friends.

* * * *

As already noted, our enthusiasm for our own sphere of activity is not always shared by our colleagues. For instance, we in the trenches frequently find the artillery of both sides unduly obtrusive; and we are of opinion that in trench warfare artillery practice should be limited by mutual consent to twelve rounds per gun per day, fired by the gunners *at* the gunners. "Except, of course, when the Big Push comes." The Big Push is seldom absent from our thoughts in these days.

"That," observed Captain Wagstaffe to Bobby Little, "would leave us foot-sloggers to settle our own differences. My opinion is that we should do so with much greater satisfaction to ourselves if we weren't constantly interfered with by coal-boxes and Black Marias."

"Still, you can't blame them for loosing off their big guns," contended the fair-minded Bobby. "It must be great sport."

"They tell me it's a greatly overrated amusement,"

replied Wagstaffe — "like posting an insulting letter to someone you dislike. You see, you aren't there when he opens it at breakfast next morning! The only man of them who gets any fun is the Forward Observing Officer. And he," concluded Wagstaffe in an unusual vein of pessimism, "does not live long enough to enjoy it!"

The grievances of the Infantry, however, are not limited to those supplied by the Royal Artillery. There are the machine-guns and the trench-mortars.

The machine-gunner is a more or less accepted nuisance by this time. He has his own emplacements in the line, but he never appears to use them. Instead, he adopts the peculiar expedient of removing his weapon from a snug and well-fortified position, and either taking it away somewhere behind the trenches and firing salvoes over your head (which is reprehensible), or planting it upon the parapet in your particular preserve, and firing it from there (which is criminal). Machine-gun fire always provokes retaliation.

"Why in thunder can't you keep your filthy tea-kettle in its own place, instead of bringing it here to draw fire?" inquired Mr Cockerell, not altogether unreasonably, as Ayling and his satellites passed along the trench bearing the offending weapon, with water-jacket aboil, back to its official residence.

"It is all for your good, my little man," explained Ayling loftily. "It would never do to give away one's real gun positions. If we did, the Boches would sit tight and say nothing at the time, but just make a note of the occurrence. Then, one fine morning, when they *really* meant business, they would begin by dropping a Black Maria on top of each emplacement; and where would you and your platoon be then, with an attack coming on and *us* out of action? So long!"

But the most unpopular man in the trenches is undoubtedly the Trench Mortar Officer. His apparatus consists of what looks like a section of rain-pipe, standing on legs. Upon its upturned muzzle is poised a bomb, having the appearance of a plum-pudding on a stick. This he discharges over the parapet into the German trenches, where it causes a comforting explosion. He then walks rapidly away.

For obvious reasons, it is not advisable to fire a trench-mortar too often — at any rate from the same place. But the whole weight of public opinion in our trench is directed against it being fired from anywhere at all. Behold the Trench Mortar Officer and his gang of pariahs creeping stealthily along in the lee of the parados, just as dawn breaks, in the section of trench occupied by No. 10 Platoon. For the moment they are unheeded, for the platoon are "standing-to", and the men are lined along the firing-step with their backs to the conspirators.

On reaching a suitable spot, the mortar party proceed to erect their apparatus with as little ostentation as possible. But they are soon discovered. The platoon subaltern hurries up.

"Awfully sorry, old man," he says breathlessly, "but the C.O. gave particular orders that this part of the trench was on no account to be used for trench-mortar fire. You see, we are only about seventy yards from the Boche trenches here —"

"I know," explains the T.M.O.; "that is why I came."

"But it is most important," continues the platoon commander, still quoting glibly from an entirely imaginary mandate of the C.O., "that no retaliatory shell fire should be attracted here. Most serious for the whole Brigade, if this bit of parapet got pushed over. Now, there a topping place about ten traverses away. You can lob them over from there beautifully. Come along."

And with fair words and honeyed phrases he elbows the dispirited band to a position — for his platoon — of comparative inoffensiveness.

The Trench Mortar Officer drifts on, and presently, with the uneasy assurance of the proprietor of a punch-and-judy show who has inadvertently strayed into Park Lane, attempts once more to give his unpopular entertainment. This time his shrift is even shorter, for he encounters Major Kemp — never at his sunniest in the small hours of the morning.

Field officers have no need to employ the language of diplomacy when dealing with subalterns.

"No, you *don't*, my lad!" announces the Major. "Not if I can help it! Take it away! Take your darned liver-pill out of this! Burn it! Bury it! Eat it! But not here! Creep away!"

The abashed procession complies. This time they find a section of trench in charge of a mere corporal. Here, before anyone of sufficient standing can be summoned to deal with the situation, the Trench Mortar Officer seizes his opportunity, and discharges three bombs over the parapet. He then retires defiantly to his dug-out.

But it is an Ishmaelitish existence.

* * * *

So much for the alleviations which professional enthusiasm bestows. Now for a few alleviations proper. There are Sleep, Food, and Literature.

Sleep is the rarest of these. We seldom get more than a few hours at a time; but it is astonishing how readily one learns to slumber in unlikely surroundings — upon damp earth, in cramped positions, amid ceaseless noise, in clothes and boots that have not been removed for days. One also acquires the priceless faculty of losing no time in dropping off.

As for food, we grumble at times, just as people at home are grumbling at the Savoy, or Lockhart's. It is the Briton's habit so to do. But in moments of repletion we are fain to confess that the organisation of our commissariat is wonderful. Of course the quality of the *menu* varies, according to the immunity of the communication trenches from shell fire, or the benevolence of the Quartermaster and the mysterious powers behind him, or the facilities for cooking offered by the time and place in which we find ourselves. No large fires are permitted: the smoke would give too good a ranging-mark to Minnie and her relatives. Still, it is surprising how quickly you can boil a canteen over a few chips. There is also, for those who can afford half-a-crown, that invaluable contrivance, "Tommy's Cooker"; and occasionally we get a ration of coke. When times are bad, we live on bully, biscuit, cheese, and water, strongly impregnated with chloride of lime. The water is conveyed to us in petrol-tins — the old familiar friends, Shell and Pratt — hundreds of them. Motorists at home must be feeling the shortage. In normal times we can reckon on plenty of hot, strong tea; possibly some bread; probably an allowance of bacon and jam. And sometimes, when the ration parties arrive, mud-stained and weary, in the dead of night, and throw down their bursting sacks, our eyes feast upon such revelations as tinned butter, condensed milk, raisins, and a consignment of that great chieftain of the ration race, The Maconochie of Maconochie. On these occasions Private Mucklewame collects his share, retires to his kennel, and has a gala-day.

Thirdly, the blessings of literature. Our letters arrive at night, with the rations. The mail of our battalion alone amounts to eight or ten mailbags a day; from which you may gather some faint idea of the labours of our Field Post Offices. There are letters, and parcels, and newspapers. Letters we may pass over. They are featureless things, except to their recipient. Parcels have more individuality. Ours are of all shapes and sizes, and most of them are astonishingly badly tied. It is quite heartrending to behold a kilted exile endeavouring to gather up a heterogeneous mess of socks, cigarettes, chocolate, soap, shortbread, and Edinburgh rock, from the ruins of what was once a flabby and unstable parcel, but is now a few skimpy rags of brown paper, which have long escaped the control of a most inadequate piece of string — a monument of maternal lavishness and feminine economy.

Then there are the newspapers. We read them right through, beginning at the advertisements and not skipping even the leading articles. Then, when we have finished, we frequently read them right through again. They serve three purposes. They give us information as to how the war is progressing — we get none here, the rank and file, that is; they serve to pass the time; and they afford us topics of conversation. For instance, they enable us to follow and discuss the trend of home politics. And in this connection, I think it is time you were introduced to Captain Achille Petitpois. (That is not his real name, but it is as near to it as most of us are likely to get.) He is one of that most efficient body, the French *liaison* officers, who act as connecting-link between the Allied Forces, and naturally is an accomplished linguist. He is an ardent admirer of British institutions, but is occasionally not a little puzzled by their complexity. So he very sensibly comes to people like Captain Wagstaffe for enlightenment, and they enlighten him.

Behold Achille — a guest in A Company's billet — drinking whisky-and-sparklet out of an aluminium mug, and discussing the news of the day.

"And your people at home," he said, "you think they are taking the War seriously?" (Achille is addicted to reading the English newspapers without discrimination.)

"So seriously," replied Wagstaffe instantly, "that it has become necessary for the Government to take steps to cheer them up."

"Comment?" inquired Achille politely.

For answer Wagstaffe picked up a three-day-old London newspaper, and read aloud an extract from the Parliamentary report. The report dealt faithfully with the latest antics of the troupe of eccentric comedians which appears (to us), since the formation of the Coalition Government, to have taken possession of the front Opposition Bench.

"Who are these assassins — these imbeciles — these *crétins*," inquired Petitpois, "who would endanger the ship of the State?" (Achille prides himself upon his knowledge of English idiom.)

"Nobody knows!" replied Wagstaffe solemnly. "They are children of mystery. Before the War, nobody had ever heard of them. They—"

"But they should be shot!" exclaimed that free-born Republican, Petitpois.

"Not a bit, old son! That is where you fail to grasp the subtleties of British statesmanship. I tell you there are no flies on our Cabinet!"

"Flies?"

"Yes: *mouches*, you know. The agility of our Cabinet Ministers is such that these little insects find it impossible to alight upon them."

"Your Ministers are athletes — yes," agreed Achille comprehendingly. "But the —"

"Only intellectually. What I mean is that they are a very downy collection of old gentlemen —"

Achille, murmuring something hazy about "Downing Street," nodded his head.

"— And when they came into power, they knew as well as anything that after three weeks or so the country would begin to grouse —"

"Grouse? A sporting bird?" interpolated Achille.

"Exactly. They knew that the country would soon start giving them the bird —"

"What bird? The grouse?"

"Oh, dry up, Wagger!" interposed Blaikie. "He means, Petitpois, that the Government, knowing that the electorate would begin to grow impatient if the War did not immediately take a favourable turn —"

Achille smiled.

"I see now," he said. "Proceed, Ouagstaffe, my old!"

"In other words," continued the officer so addressed, "the Government decided that if they gave the Opposition half a chance to get together, and find leaders, and consolidate their new trenches, they might turn them out."

"Bien," assented Achille. Every one was listening now, for Wagstaffe as a politician usually had something original to say.

"Well," proceeded Wagstaffe, "they saw that the great thing to do was to prevent the Opposition from making an impression on the country — from being taken too seriously, in fact. So what did they do? They said: 'Let's arrange for a *comic* Opposition — an Opposition *pour rire*, you know. They will make the country either laugh or cry. Anyhow, the country will be much too busy deciding which to do to have any time to worry about *us*; so we shall have a splendid chance to get on with the War.' So they sent down the Strand — that's where the Variety agents foregather, I believe — what you call *entrepreneurs*, Achille — and booked this troupe, complete, for the run of the War. They did the thing in style; spared no expense; and got a comic newspaper proprietor to write the troupe up, and themselves down. The scheme worked beautifully — what you would call a *succès fou*, Achille."

"I am desolated, my good Ouagstaffe," observed Petitpois after a pregnant silence; "but I cannot believe all you say."

"I *may* be wrong," admitted Wagstaffe handsomely, "but that's my reading of the situation. At any rate,

Achille, you will admit that my theory squares with the known facts of the case."

Petitpois bowed politely.

"Perhaps it is I who am wrong, my dear Ouagger. There is such a difference of point of view between your politics and ours."

The deep voice of Captain Blaikie broke in.

"If Lancashire," he said grimly, "were occupied by a German army, as the Lille district is today, I fancy there would be a considerable levelling up of political points of view all round. No limelight for a comic opposition then, Achille, old son!"

*   *   *   *

Besides receiving letters, we write them. And this brings us to that mysterious and impalpable despot, the Censor.

There is not much mystery about him really. Like a good many other highly placed individuals, he deputes as much of his work as possible to someone else — in this case that long-suffering maid-of-all-work, the company officer. Let us track Bobby Little to his dug-out, during one of those numerous periods of enforced retirement which occur between the hours of three and six, "Pip Emma" — as our friends the "buzzers" call the afternoon. On the floor of this retreat (which looks like a dog-kennel and smells like a vault) he finds a small heap of letters, deposited there for purposes of what the platoon sergeant calls "censure". These have to be read (which is bad); licked up (which is far worse); signed on the outside by the officer, and forwarded to Headquarters. Here they are stamped with the familiar red triangle and forwarded to the Base, where they are supposed to be scrutinised by the real Censor — *i.e.,* the gentleman who is paid for the job — and are finally de-spatched to their destination.

Bobby, drawing his legs well inside the kennel, out of the way of stray shrapnel bullets, begins his task.

The heap resolves itself into three parts. First come the postcards, which give no trouble, as their secrets are written plain for all to see. There are half a dozen or so of the British Army official issue, which are designed for the benefit of those who lack the epistolatory gift — what would a woman say if you offered such things to her? — and bear upon the back the following printed statements:

I am quite well.
I have been admitted to hospital.
I am sick } { *and am going on well.*
wounded } { *and hope to be discharged soon.*
I have received your (*letter,   dated . . .*
{ *telegram,   „*
(*parcel   „*
Letter follows at first opportunity.
I have received no letter from you (*lately.*
{ *for a long time.*

(The gentleman who designed this postcard must have been a descendant of Sydney Smith. You remember that great man's criticism of the Books of Euclid? He preferred the Second Book, on the ground that it was more "impassioned" than the others!)

All the sender of this impassioned missive has to do to delete such clauses as strike him as untruthful or over-demonstrative, and sign his name. He is not allowed to add any comments of his own. On this occasion, however, one indignant gentleman has pencilled the ironical phrase, "I don't think!" opposite the line which acknowledges the receipt of a parcel. Bobby lays this aside, to be returned to the sender.

Then come some French picture postcards. Most of these present soldiers — soldiers posing, soldiers exchanging international handgrips, soldiers grouped round a massive and *décolletée* lady in flowing robes, and declaring that *La patrie sera libre!* Underneath this last, Private Ogg has written: "Dear Lizzie, — I hope this finds you well as it leaves me so. I send you a French p.c. The writing means long live the Queen of France."

The next heap consists of letters in official-looking green envelopes. These are already sealed up, and the sender has signed the following attestation, printed on the flap: *I certify on my honour that the contents of this envelope refer to nothing but private and family matters.* Setting aside a rather bulky epistle addressed the The Editor of a popular London weekly, which advertises a circulation of over a million copies — a singularly unsuitable recipient for correspondence of a private and family nature — Bobby turns to the third heap, and sets to work upon his daily task of detecting items of information, "which if intercepted or published might prove of value to the enemy".

It is not a pleasant task to pry into another person's correspondence, but Bobby's scruples are considerably abated by the consciousness that on this occaison he is doing so with the writer's full knowledge. Consequently it is a clear case of *caveat scriptor*. Not that Bobby's flock show any embarrassment at the prospect of his scrutiny. Most of them write with the utmost frankness, whether they are conducting a love affair, or are involved in a domestic broil of the most personal nature. In fact, they seem rather to enjoy having an official audience. Others cheerfully avail themselves of this opportunity of conveying advice or reproof to those above them, by means of what the Royal Artillery call "indirect fire". Private Dunshie remarks: "We have been getting no pay these three weeks, but I doubt the officer will know what has become of the money." It is the firm conviction of every private soldier in "K(1)" that all fines and deductions go straight into the pocket of the officer who levies them. Private Hogg, always an optimist, opines: "The officers should know better how to treat us now, for they all get a read of our letters."

But, as recorded above, the outstanding feature of this correspondence is an engaging frankness. For instance, Private Cosh, who under an undemonstrative, not to say wooden, exterior evidently conceals a heart as inflammable as flannelette, is conducting single-handed no less than four parallel love affairs. One lady resides in his native Coatbridge, the second is in service in South Kensington, the third serves in a shop in Kelvinside, and the fourth moth appears to have been attracted to this most unlikely candle during our sojourn in winter billets in Hampshire. Cosh writes to them all most ardently every week — sometimes oftener — and Bobby Little, as he ploughs wearily through repeated demands for photographs, and touching protestations of lifelong affection, curses the verbose and susceptible youth with all his heart.

But this mail brings him a gleam of comfort.

So you tell me, Chrissie, writes Cosh to the lady in South Kensington, *that you are engaged to be married on a milkman. . . .*

("Thank heaven!" murmurs Bobby piously.)

No, no, Chrissie, you need not trouble yourself. It is nothing to me.

("He's as sick as muck!" comments Bobby.)

All I did before was in friendship's name.

("Liar!")

Bobby, thankfully realising that his daily labours will be materially lightened by the withdrawal of the fickle Chrissie from the postal arena, ploughs steadily through the letters. Most of them begin in accordance with some approved formula, such as —

It is with the greatest of pleasure that I take up my pen —

It is invariably a pencil, and a blunt one at that.

Crosses are ubiquitous, and the flap of the envelope usually bears the mystic formula, S.W.A.K. This apparently means "Sealed with a kiss," which, considering that the sealing is done not by the writer but by the Censor, seems to take a good deal for granted.

Most of the letters acknowledge the receipt of a "parcel"; many give a guarded summary of the military situation.

We are not allowed to tell you about the War, but I may say that we are now in the trenches. We are all in the pink, and not many of the boys has gotten a dose of lead-poisoning yet.

It is a pity that the names of places have to be left blank. Otherwise we should get some fine phonetic spelling. Our pronunciation is founded on no pedantic rules. Armentières is Armentears, Busnes is Business, Bailleul is Booloo, and Vieille Chapelle is Veal Chapel.

The chief difficulty of the writers appears to be to round off their letters gracefully. *Having no more to say, I will now draw to a close,* is the accepted formula. Private Burke, never a tactician, concludes a most ardent love-letter thus: *"Well, Kate, I will now close, as I have to write to another of the girls."*

But to Private Mucklewame literary composition presents no difficulties. Here is a single example of his terse and masterly style:

Dere wife, if you could make the next postal order a trifle stronger, I might get getting an egg to my tea. — Your loving husband, JAS. MUCKLEWAME, *No.* 74077.

But there are features of this multifarious correspondence over which one has no inclination to smile. There are wistful references to old days; tender inquiries after bairns and weans; assurances to anxious wives and mothers that the dangers of modern warfare are merely nominal. There is an almost entire absence of boasting or lying, and very little complaining. There is a general and obvious desire to allay anxiety. We are all "fine"; we are all "in the pink". "This is a grand life."

Listen to Lance-Corporal McSnape: *Well, mother, I got your parcel, and the things was most welcome; but you must not send any more. I seen a shilling stamp on the parcel: that is too much for you to afford.* How many officers take the trouble to examine the stamp on their parcels?

And there is a wealth of homely sentiment and honest affection which holds up its head without shame even in the presence of the Censor. One rather pathetic screed, beginning: *Well, wife, I doubt this will be a poor letter, for I canna get one of they green envelopes today, but I'll try my best* — Bobby Little sealed and signed without further scrutiny.

*   *   *   *

One more picture, to close the record of our trivial round.

It is a dark, moist, and most unpleasant dawn, Captain Blaikie stands leaning against a traverse in the fire-trench, superintending the return of a party from picket duty. They file in, sleepy and dishevelled, through an archway in the parapet, on their way to dug-outs and repose. The last man in the procession is Bobby Little, who has been in charge all night.

Our line here makes a sharp bend round the corner of an orchard, and for security's sake a second trench has been cut behind, making, as it were, the cross-bar for a capital A. The apex of the A is no health resort. Brother Boche, as already explained, is only fifty yards away, and his trench-mortars make excellent practice with the parapet. So the Orchard Trench is only occupied at night, and the alternative route, which is well constructed and comparatively safe, is used by all careful persons who desire to proceed from one arm of the A to the other.

The present party are the night picket, thankfully relinquishing their vigil round the apex.

Bobby Little remained to bid his company commander good-morning at the junction of the two trenches.

"Any casualties?" An invariable question at this spot.

"No, sir. We were lucky. There was a lot of sniping."

"It's a rum profession," mused Captain Blaikie, who was in a wakeful mood.

"In what way, sir?" inquired the sleepy but respectful Bobby.

"Well" — Captain Blaikie began to fill his pipe — "who takes about nine-tenths of the risk, and does practically all the hard work in the Army? The private and the subaltern — you and your picket, in fact. Now, here is the problem which has puzzled me ever since I joined the Army, and I've had nineteen years' service. The farther away you remove the British soldier from the risk of personal injury, the higher you pay him. Out here, a private of the line gets about a shilling a day. For that he digs, saps, marches, and fights like a hero. The motor-transport driver gets six shillings a day, no danger, and lives like a fighting cock. The Army Service Corps drive about in motors, pinch our rations, and draw princely incomes. Staff Officers are compensated for their comparative security by extra cash, and first chop at the war medals. Now — why?"

"I dare say they would sooner be here, in the trenches, with us," was Bobby's characteristic reply.

Blaikie lit his pipe — it was almost broad daylight now — and considered.

"Yes," he agreed — "perhaps. Still, my son, I can't say I have ever noticed Staff Officers crowding into the trenches (as they have a perfect right to do) at four o'clock in the morning. And I can't say I altogether blame them. In fact, if ever I do meet one performing such a feat, I shall say: 'There goes a sahib — and a soldier!' and I shall take off my hat to him."

"Well, get ready now," said Bobby. "Look!"

They were still standing at the trench junction. Two figures, in the uniform of the Staff, were visible in Orchard Trench, working their way down from the apex — picking their steps amid the tumbled sandbags, and stooping low to avoid gaps in the ruined parapet. The sun was just rising behind the German trenches. One of the officers was burly and middle-aged; he did not appear to enjoy bending double. His companion was slight, fair-haired, and looked incredibly young. Once or twice he glanced over his shoulder, and smiled encouragingly at his senior.

The pair emerged through the archway into the main trench, and straightened their backs with obvious relief. The younger officer — he was a lieutenant — noticed Captain Blaikie, saluted him gravely, and turned to follow his companion.

Captain Blaikie did not take his hat off, as he had promised. Instead, he stood suddenly to attention, and saluted in return, keeping his hand uplifted until the slim, childish figure had disappeared round the corner of a traverse.

It was the Prince of Wales.

CHAPTER TWENTY

THE GATHERING
OF THE EAGLES

WHEN THIS WAR is over, and the glory and the praise
are duly assigned, particularly honourable mention
should be made of the inhabitants of a certain ancient
French town with a Scottish name, which lies not far
behind a particularly sultry stretch of the trenches. The
town is subject to shell fire, as splintered walls and shattered windows testify; yet every shop stands open. The
town, moreover, is the only considerable place in the
district, and enjoys a monopoly of patronage from all
the surrounding billeting areas; yet the keepers of the
shops have heroically refrained from putting up their
prices to any appreciable extent. This combination of
courage and fair-dealing has had its reward. The town
has become a local Mecca. British soldiers with an
afternoon to spare and a few francs to spend come in
from miles around. Mess presidents send in their mess-
sergeants, and fearful and wonderful is the marketing
which ensues.

In remote and rural billets catering is a simple matter. We take what we can get, and leave it at that. The
following business-card, which Bobby Little once
found attached to an outhouse door in one of his bil-

lets, puts the resources of a French hamlet into a nut-shell:

HÉRE
SMOKINÒ ROM
BÉER
WINE ⎰ WITHE
⎱ RAID
COFFÉ
EGS

But in town the shopper has a wider range. Behold Sergeant Goffin, a true-born Londoner, with the Londoner's faculty of never being at a loss for a word, at the grocer's purchasing comforts for our Officers' Mess.

"Bong jooer, Mrs Pankhurst!" he observes breezily to the plump *épicière*. This is his invariable greeting to French ladies who display any tendency to volubility — and they are many.

"Bon jour, M'sieu le Caporal!" replies the *épicière*, smiling. "M'sieu le Caporal désire?"

The sergeant allows his reduction in rank to pass unnoticed. He does not understand the French tongue, though he speaks it with great fluency and incredible success. He holds up a warning hand.

"Now, keep your 'and off the tap of the gas meter for one minute *if* you please," he rejoins, "and let me get a word in edgeways. I want" — with great emphasis — "vinblank one, vinrooge two, bogeys six, Dom one. Compree?"

By some miracle the smiling lady does "compree", and produces white wine, red wine, candles, and — a bottle of Benedictine! (Sergeant Goffin always names wines after the most boldly printed work upon the label. He once handed round some champagne, which he insisted on calling "a bottle of brute".)

"Combine?" is the next observation.

The *épicière* utters the series of short sharp sibilants

of which all French numerals appear to be composed. It sounds like "song-song-song". The resourceful Goffin lays down a twenty-franc note.

"Take it out of that," he says grandly.

He receives his change, and counts it with a great air of wisdom. The *épicière* breaks into a rapid recital — it sounds rather like our curate at home getting to work on *When the wicked man* — of the beauty and succulence of her other wares. Up goes Goffin's hand again.

"Na pooh!" he exclaims. "Bong jooer!" And he stumps out to the mess-cart.

"Na pooh!" is a mysterious but invaluable expression. Possibly it is derived from "Il n'y a plus". It means, "All over!" You say "Na pooh!" when you push your plate away after dinner. It also means, "Not likely!" or "Nothing doing!" By a further development it has come to mean "done for", "finished", and in extreme cases, "dead". "Poor Bill got napoohed by a rifle-grenade yesterday," says one mourner to another.

The Oxford Dictionary of the English Language will have to be revised and enlarged when this war is over.

Meanwhile, a few doors away, a host of officers is sitting in the Café de la Terre. Cafés are as plentiful as blackberries in this, as in most other French provincial towns, and they are usually filled to overflowing with privates of the British Army heroically drinking beer upon which they know it is impossible to get intoxicated. But the proprietor of the Café de la Terre is a long-headed citizen. By the simple expedient of labelling his premises "Officers Only", and making a minimum charge of one franc per drink, he has at a single stroke ensured the presence of the *élite* and increased his profits tenfold.

Many arms of the Service are grouped round the little marble-topped tables, for the district is stiff with

British troops, and promises to grow stiffer. In fact, so persistently are the eagles gathering together upon this, the edge of the fighting line, that rumour is busier than ever. The Big Push holds redoubled sway in our thoughts. The First Hundred Thousand are well represented, for the whole Scottish Division is in the neighbourhood. Beside the glengarries there are countless flat caps — line regiments, territorials, gunners, and sappers. The Army Service Corps is there in force, recruiting exhausted nature from the strain of dashing about the countryside in motor-cars. The R.A.M.C. is strongly represented, doubtless to test the purity of the refreshment provided. Even the Staff has torn itself away from its arduous duties for the moment, as sundry red tabs testify. In one corner sit four stout French civilians, playing a mysterious card-game.

At the very next table we find ourselves among friends. Here are Major Kemp, also Captain Blaikie. They are accompanied by Ayling, Bobby Little, and Mr Waddell. The battalion came out of trenches yesterday, and for the first time found itself in urban billets. For the moment haylofts and wash-houses are things of the dim past. We are living in real houses, sleeping in real beds, some with sheets.

To this group enters unexpectedly Captain Wagstaffe.

"Hallo, Wagger!" says Blaikie. "Back already?"

"Your surmise is correct," replies Wagstaffe, who has been home on leave. "I got a wire yesterday at lunch-time — in the Savoy, of all places! Everyone on leave has been recalled. We were packed like herrings on the boat. Garçon, bière — the brunette kind!"

"Tell us all about London," says Ayling hungrily. "What does it look like? Tell us!"

We have been out here for the best part of five months now. Leave opened a fortnight ago, amid acclamations — only to be closed again within a few days. Wagstaffe was one of the lucky few who slipped through the blessed portals. He now sips his beer and delivers his report.

"London is much as usual. A bit rattled over Zeppelins — they have turned out even more street lamps — but nothing to signify. Country districts crawling with troops. All the officers appear to be colonels. Promotion at home is more rapid than out here. Chin, chin!" Wagstaffe buries his face in his glass mug.

"What is the general attitude," asked Mr Waddell, "towards the war?"

"Well, one's own friends are down in the dumps. Of course it's only natural, because most of them are in mourning. Our losses are much more noticeable at home than abroad, somehow. People seemed quite surprised when I told them that things out here are as right as rain, and that our troops are simply tumbling over one another, and that we don't require any comic M.P.'s sent out to cheer us up. The fact is, some people read the papers too much. At the present moment the London press is, not to put too fine a point on it, making a holy show of itself. I suppose there's some low-down political rig at the back of it all, but the whole business must be perfect jam for the Boches in Berlin."

"What's the trouble?" inquired Major Kemp.

"Conscription, mostly. (Though why they should worry their little heads about it, I don't know. If K. wants it we'll have it: if not, we won't; so that's that!) Both sides are trying to drag the great British Public into the scrap by the back of the neck. The Conscription crowd, with whom one would naturally side if they would play the game, seem to be out to unseat the Government as a preliminary. They support their arguments by stating that the British Army on the Western front is reduced to a few platoons, and that they are allowed to fire one shell per day. At least, that's what I gathered."

"What do the other side say?" inquired Kemp.

"Oh, theirs is a very simple line of argument. They state, quite simply, that if the personal liberty of Britain's workers — that doesn't mean you and me, as you might think: we are the Overbearing Militarist Oligarchy: a worker is a man who goes on strike — they say that if the personal liberty of these sacred perishers is interfered with by the Overbearing Militarist Oligarchy aforesaid, there will be a Revolution. That's all! Oh, they're a sweet lot, the British newspaper bosses!"

"But what," inquired that earnest seeker after knowledge, Mr Waddell, "is the general attitude of the country at large upon this grave question?"

Captain Wagstaffe chuckled.

"The dear old country at large," he replied, "is its dear old self, as usual. It is not worrying one jot about Conscription, or us, or anything like that. The one topic of conversation at present is — Charlie Chaplin."

"Who is Charlie Chaplin?" inquired several voices.

Wagstaffe shook his head.

"I haven't the faintest idea," he said. "All I know is that you can't go anywhere in London without running up against him. He is It. The mention of his name in a *revue* is greeted with thunders of applause. At one place I went to, twenty young men came upon the stage at once, all got up as Charlie Chaplin."

"But who *is* he?"

"That I can't tell you. I made several attempts to find out; but whenever I asked the question people simply stared at me in amazement. I felt quite ashamed: it was plain that I ought to have known. I have a vague idea that he is some tremendous new boss whom the Government have appointed to make shells, or something. Anyhow, the great British Nation is far too much engrossed with Charles to worry about a little thing like Conscription. Still, I should like to know. I feel I have been rather unpatriotic about it all."

"I can tell you," said Bobby Little. "My servant is a great admirer of his. He is the latest cinema star. Falls off roofs, and gets run over by motors —"

"And keeps the police at bay with a fire-hose," added Wagstaffe. "That's him! I know the type. Thank you, Bobby!"

Major Kemp put down his glass with a gentle sigh, and rose to go.

"We are a great nation," he remarked contentedly. "I was a bit anxious about things at home, but I see now there was nothing to worry about. We shall win all right. Well, I am off to the Mess. See you later, everybody!"

"Meanwhile," inquired Wagstaffe, as the party settled down again, "what is brewing here? I haven't seen the adjutant yet."

"You'll see him soon enough," replied Blaikie grimly. He glanced over his shoulder towards the four civilian card-players. They looked bourgeois enough and patriotic enough, but it is wise to take no risks in a café, as a printed notice upon the wall, signed by the Provost-Marshal, was careful to point out. "Come for a stroll," he said.

Presently the two captains found themselves in a shady boulevard leading to the outskirts of the town. Darkness was falling, and soon would be intense; for lights are taboo in the neighbourhood of the firing line.

"Have we finished that new trench in front of our wire?" asked Wagstaffe.

"Yes. It is the best thing we have done yet. Divisional Headquarters are rightly pleased about it."

Blaikie gave details. The order had gone forth that a new trench was to be constructed in front of our present line — a hundred yards in front. Accordingly, when night fell, two hundred unconcerned heroes went forth, under their subalterns, and, squatting down in line along a white tape (laid earlier in the evening by our imperturbable friends, Lieutenants Box and Cox, of the Royal Engineers), proceeded to dig the trench. Thirty yards ahead of them, facing the curious eyes of countless Boches, lay a covering party in extended order, ready to repel a rush. Hour by hour the work went on — skilfully, silently. On these occasions it is impossible to say what will happen. The enemy knows we are there: he can see us quite plainly. But he has his own night-work to do, and if he interferes with us he knows that our machine-guns will interfere with him. So, provided that our labours are conducted in a manner which is neither ostentatious nor contemptuous — that is to say, provided we do not talk, whistle, or smoke — he leaves us more or less alone.

But this particular task was not accomplished without loss: it was too obviously important. Several times the German machine-guns sputtered into flame, and each time the stretcher-bearers were called upon to do their duty. Yet the work went on to its accomplishment, without question, without slackening. The men were nearly all experts: they had handled pick and shovel from boyhood. Soldiers of the line would have worked quite as hard, maybe, but they would have taken twice as long. But these dour sons of Scotland worked like giants — trained giants. In four nights the trench, with traverses and approaches, was complete. The men who had made it fell back to their dug-outs, and shortly afterwards to their billets — there to spend the few odd francs which their separation allotments had left them, upon extremely hard-earned glasses of extremely small beer.

At home, several thousand patriotic Welshmen, fellows of the same craft, were upholding the dignity of Labour, and the reputation of the British Nation, by going out on strike for a further increase of pay — an increase which they knew a helpless Government would grant them. It was one of the strangest contrasts that the world has ever seen. But the explanation thereof, as proffered by Private Mucklewame, was quite simple and eminently sound.

"All the decent lads," he observed briefly, "are oot here."

"Good work!" said Wagstaffe, when Blaikie's tale was told. "What is the new trench for, exactly?"

Blaikie told him.

"Tell me more!" urged Wagstaffe, deeply interested.

Blaikie's statement cannot be set down here, though the substance of it may be common property today. When he had finished Wagstaffe whistled softly.

"And it's to be the day after tomorrow?" he said.

"Yes, if all goes well."

It was quite dark now. The horizon was brilliantly lit by the flashes of big guns, and a continuous roar came throbbing through the soft autumn darkness.

"If this thing goes with a click, as it ought to do," said Wagstaffe, "it will be the biggest thing that ever happened — bigger even than Charlie Chaplin."

"Yes — *if!*" assented the cautious Blaikie.

"It's a tremendous opportunity for our section of 'K(1),'" continued Wagstaffe. "We shall have a chance of making history over this, old man."

"Whatever we make — history or a bloomer — we'll do our level best," replied Blaikie. "At least, I hope 'A' Company will."

Then suddenly his reserved, undemonstrative Scottish tongue found utterance.

"Scotland for Ever!" he cried softly.

CHAPTER TWENTY-ONE

THE BATTLE
OF THE SLAG-HEAPS

"HALF-PAST TWO, and a cold morning, sir."

Thus Bobby Little's servant, rousing his employer from uneasy slumber under the open sky, in a newly-constructed trench running parallel to and in rear of the permanent trench line.

Bobby sat up, and peering at his luminous wrist-watch, morosely acquiesced in his menial's gruesome statement. But he cheered up at the next intimation.

"Breakfast is ready, sir."

Tea and bacon are always tea and bacon, even in the gross darkness and mental tension which precede a Big Push. Presently various humped figures in greatcoats, having gathered in the open ditch which did duty for Officers' Mess, broke into spasmodic conversation — conversation rendered even more spasmodic by the almost ceaseless roar of guns. There were guns all round us — rank upon rank: to judge by the noise, you would have said tier upon tier as well. Half a mile ahead, upon the face of a gentle slope, a sequence of flames would spout from the ground, and a storm of shells go whistling on their way. No sooner had this happened than there would come a shattering roar from the ground beneath our feet, and a heavy battery, concealed in a hedge fifty yards to our front, would launch its contribution. Farther back lay heavier batteries still, and beyond that batteries so powerful and so distant that one heard the shell pass before the report arrived. One of these monsters, coming apparently from infinity and bound for the back of beyond, lumbered wearily over the head of "A" Company, partaking of breakfast.

Private Mucklewame paused in the act of raising his canteen to his lips.

"There's Wullie awa' for a walk!" he observed.

Considering that they were upon the eve of an epoch-making combat, the regiment were disappointingly placid.

In the Officers' Mess the prevailing note was neither lust of battle nor fear of death: it was merely that ordinary snappishness which is induced by early rising and uncomfortable surroundings.

"It's going to rain, too," grumbled Major Kemp.

At this moment the Colonel arrived, with final instructions from the Brigadier.

"We move off at a quarter to four," he said, "up Fountain Alley and Scottish Trench, into Central Boyau" — "boyau" is the name which is given to a communication trench in trenches which, like those in front of us, are of French extraction — "and so over the parapet. There we extend, as arranged, into lines of half-companies, and go at 'em, making Douvrin our objective, and keeping the Hohenzollern and Fosse Eight upon our left."

Fosse Eight is a mighty waste-heap, such as you may behold anywhere along the railway in the colliery districts between Glasgow and Edinburgh. The official map calls such an eminence a Fosse; the Royal Engineers call it a Dump; Operation Orders call it a Slag-Heap; experts like Ogg and Hogg (who ought to know if anyone does) call it a Bing. From this distance, two miles away, the Fosse looks as big as North Berwick Law. It is one of the many scattered about this district, all carefully numbered by the Ordnance. There are others, again, towards Hulluch and Loos. Number Eight has been the object of pressing attentions on the part of our big guns ever since the bombardment began, three weeks ago; but it still stands up — gaunt, grim, and defiant — against the eastern sky. Whether anyone is left alive upon it, or in it, is another question. We shall have cause to remember Fosse Eight before this fight is over.

The Hohenzollern Redoubt, on the other hand, is a most inconspicuous object, but a very important factor in the present situation. It has been thrust forward from the Boche lines to within a hundred yards of our own — a great promontory, a maze of trenches, machine-gun emplacements, and barbed wire, all flush with or under the ground, and terribly difficult to cripple by shell fire. It has been a source of great exasperation to us — a starting-point for saps, mines, and bombing parties. As already stated, this mighty fortress has been christened by its constructors, the Hohenzollern. It is attached to its parent trench-line by two communicating trenches, which the British Army, not to be outdone in reverence to the most august of dynasties, have named Big and Little Willie respectively.

A struggling dawn breaks, bringing with it promise of rain, and the regiment begins to marshal in the trench called Fountain Alley, along which it is to wind, snake-like, in the wake of the preceding troops, until it debouches over the parapet, a full mile away, and extends into line.

Presently the order is given to move off, and the snake begins to writhe. Progress is steady, but not exhilarating. We have several batallions of the Division in front of us (which Bobby Little resents as a personal affront), but have been assured that we shall see all the fighting we want. The situation appears to be that owing to the terrific artillery bombardment the attacking force will meet with little or no opposition in the German front-line trenches; or second line, for that matter.

"The whole Division," explains Captain Wagstaffe to Bobby Little, "should be able to get up into some sort of formation about the Boche third line before any real fighting begins; so it does not very much matter whether we start first or fiftieth in the procession."

Captain Wagstaffe showed himself an accurate prophet.

We move on. At one point we pass through a howitzer battery, where dishevelled gentlemen give us a friendly wave of the hand. Others, not professionally engaged for the moment, sit unconcernedly in the ditch with their backs to the proceedings, frying bacon. This is their busy hour.

Presently the pace grows even slower, and finally we stop altogether. Another battalion has cut in ahead of us, and we must perforce wait, snapping our fingers with impatience, like theatre-goers in a Piccadilly block, whose taxis have been held up by the traffic debouching from Berkeley Street.

"Luckily the curtain doesn't rise till five-fifty," observes Captain Wagstaffe.

We move on again at last, and find ourselves in Central Boyau, getting near the heart of things. Suddenly we are conscious of an over-powering sense of relief. Our guns have ceased firing. For the first time for three days and nights there is peace.

Captain Wagstaffe looks at his watch.

"That means that our first line are going over the parapet," he says. "Punctual, too! The gunners have stopped to put up their sights and lengthen their fuses. We ought to be fairly in it in half an hour."

But this proves to be an under-estimate. There are

mysterious and maddening stoppages — maddening, because in communication-trench stoppages it is quite impossible to find out what is the matter. Furious messages begin to arrive from the rear. The original form of inquiry was probably something like this: "Major Kemp would like to know the cause of the delay." As transmitted sonorously from mouth to mouth by the rank and file, it finally arrives (if it ever arrives at all) in some such words as: "Pass doon; what for is this (asterisk, obelus) wait?" But as no answer is ever passed back it does not much matter.

The righteous indignation of Major Kemp, who is situated somewhere about the middle of the procession, reaches its culminating point when, with much struggling and pushing and hopeless jamming, a stretcher carrying a wounded man is borne down the crowded trench on its way to the rear. The Major delivers himself.

"This is perfectly monstrous! You stretcher-bearers will kill that poor chap if you try to drag him down here. There is a specially constructed road to the dressing-station over there — Bart's Alley, it is called. We cannot have up-and-down traffic jumbled together like this. For heaven's sake, Waddell, pass up word to the C.O. that it is mistaken kindness to allow these fellows down here. He *must* send them back."

Waddell volunteers to climb out of the trench and go forward with a message. But this the Major will not allow. "Your platoon will require a leader presently," he mentions. "We'll try the effect of a note."

The note is passed up, and anon an answer comes back to the effect that no wounded have been allowed down from the head of the column. They must be getting in by a side-track somewhere. The Major groans, but can do nothing.

Presently there is a fresh block.

"What is it this time?" inquires the afflicted Kemp.

"More wounded, or are we being photographed?"

The answer races joyously down the line —

"Gairman prisoners, sirr — seeventy of them!"

This time the Major acts with promptness and decision.

"Prisoners? No, they *don't!* Pass up word from me that the whole boiling are to be hoisted on to the parapet, with their escort, and made to walk above ground."

The order goes forward. Presently our hearts are rejoiced by an exhilarating sight. Across the field through which our trench winds comes a body of men, running rapidly, encouraged to further fleetness of foot by desultory shrapnel and stray bullets. They wear grey-green uniform, and flat, muffin-shaped caps. They have no arms or equipment: some are slightly wounded. In front of this contingent, running even more rapidly, are their escort — some dozen brawny Highlanders, armed to the teeth. But the prisoners exhibit no desire to take advantage of this unusual order of things. Their one ambition in life appears to be to put as large a space as possible between themselves and their late comrades-in-arms, and, if possible, overtake their captors.

Some of them find time to grin, and wave their hands to us. One addresses the scandalised McSlattery as "Kamerad!" "No more dis war for me" cries another, with unfeigned satisfaction.

After this our progress is more rapid. As we near the front line, the enemy's shrapnel reaps its harvest even in our deep trench. More than once we pass a wounded man, hoisted on to the parapet to wait for first-aid. More than once we step over some poor fellow for whom no first-aid will avail.

Five minutes later we reach the parapet — that immovable rampart over which we have peeped so often and so cautiously with our periscopes — and clamber up a sandbag staircase on to the summit. We note that our barbed wire has all been cut away, and that another battalion, already extended into line, is advancing fifty yards ahead of us. Bullets are pinging through the air, but the guns are once more silent. Possibly they are altering their position. Dotted about upon the flat ground before us lie many kilted figures, strangely still, in uncomfortable attitudes.

A mile or so upon our right we can see two towers — pit-head towers — standing side by side. They mark the village of Loos, where another Scottish Division is leading the attack. To the right of Loos again, for miles and miles and miles, we know that wave upon wave of impetuous French soldiers is breaking in a tempest over the shattered German trenches. Indeed, we conjecture that down there, upon our right, is where the Biggest Push of all is taking place. Our duty is to get forward if we can, but before everything to engage as many German troops and guns as possible. Even if we fight for a week or more, and only hold our own, we shall have done the greater part of what was required of us. But we hope to do more than that.

Upon our left lies the Hohenzollern. It is silent; so we know that it has been captured. Beyond that, upon our left front, looms Fosse Eight, still surmounted by its battered shaft-tower. Right ahead, peeping over a low ridge, is a church steeple, with a clock-face in it. That is our objective.

Next moment we have deployed into extended order, and step out, to play our little part in the great Battle of the Slag-Heaps.

*   *   *   *

Twenty-four hours later, a little group of officers sat in a roomy dug-out. Major Kemp was there, with his head upon the plank table, fast asleep. Bobby Little, who had neither eaten nor slept since the previous dawn, was nibbling chocolate and shaking as if with ague. He had gone through a good deal. Waddell sat opposite to him, stolidly devouring bully beef out of a tin with his fingers. Ayling reclined upon the floor, mechanically adjusting a machine-gun lock, which he had taken from his haversack. Captain Wagstaffe was making cocoa over a Tommy's Cooker. He looked less the worse for wear than the others, but could hardly have been described as spruce in appearance. The whole party were splashed with mud and soaked to the skin, for it had rained hard during the greater part of the night. They were all sick for want of food and sleep. Moreover, all had seen unusual sights. It was Sunday morning.

Presently Wagstaffe completed his culinary arrangements, and poured out the cocoa into some aluminium cups. He touched Major Kemp on the shoulder.

"Have some of this, Major," he said.

The burly Kemp roused himself and took the proffered cup gratefully. Then, looking round, he said —

"Hallo, Ayling! You arrived? Whereabouts in the line were you?"

"I got cut off from the Battalion in the advance up Central Boyau, sir," said Ayling. "Everybody had disappeared by the time I got the machine-guns over the parapet. However, knowing the objective, I pushed on towards the Church Tower."

"How did you enjoy yourself passing Fosse Eight?" inquired Captain Wagstaffe.

"Thank you, we got a dose of our own medicine — machine-gun fire, in enfilade. It was beastly."

"We also noticed it," Wagstaffe intimated. "That was where poor Sinclair got knocked out. What did you do?"

"I signalled to the men to lie flat for a bit, and did the same. I did not know that it was possible for a human being to lie as flat as I lay during that quarter of an hour.

But it was no good. The guns must have been high up on the Fosse: they had excellent command. The bullets simply greased all round us. I could feel them combing out my hair, and digging into the ground underneath me."

"What were your sensations, *exactly?*" asked Kemp.

"I felt just as if an invisible person were tickling me," replied Ayling, with feeling.

"So did I," said Kemp. "Go on."

"I heard one of my men cry out that he was hit," continued Ayling, "and I came to the conclusion that we would have a better chance as moving targets than as fixed; so I passed the word to get up and move forward steadily, in single file. Ultimately we struck a stray communication trench, into which we descended with as much dignity as possible. It led us into some quarries."

"Off our line altogether."

"So I learned from two Companies of an English regiment which were there, acting as reserve to a Brigade which was scrapping somewhere in the direction of Hulluch; so I realised that we had worked too far to the right. We moved out of the quarries and struck over half-left, and ultimately found the Battalion, a very long way ahead, in what I took to be a Boche third-line trench, facing east."

"Right! Fosse Alley," said Kemp. "You remember it on the map?"

"Yes, I do now," said Ayling. "Well, I planted myself on the right flank of the Battalion with two guns, and sent Sergeant Killick along with the other two to the left. You know the rest."

"I'm not sure that I do," said the Major. "We were packed so tight in that blooming trench that it was quite impossible to move about, and I only saw what was going on close around me. Did you get much machine-gun practice?"

"A fair amount, sir," replied Ayling, with professional satisfaction. "There was a lot of firing from our right front, so I combed out all the bushes and house-fronts I could see; and presently the firing died down, but not before I had had one gun put out of action with a bullet through the barrel-casing. After dark things were fairly quiet, except for constant alarms, until the order came to move back to the next trench."

Major Kemp's fist came down upon the plank table.

"Move back!" he exclaimed angrily. "Just so! To capture Fosse Alley, hold it all day and half the night, and then be compelled to move back, simply because we had pushed so far ahead of any other Division that we had no support on either flank! It was tough — rotten — hellish! Excuse my exuberance. You all right, Wagstaffe?"

"Wonderful, considering," replied Wagstaffe. "I was mildly gassed by a lachrymous shell about two o'clock this morning, but nothing to signify."

"Did your respirator work?"

"I found that in the heat of the moment I had mislaid it."

"What did you do?"

"I climbed on to the parapet and sat there. It seemed the healthiest spot under the circumstances: anyhow, the air was pure. When I recovered I got down. What happened to 'A', Bobby? I heard rumours, but hoped —"

He hesitated.

"Go on," he said abruptly, and Bobby, more composed now, told his tale.

"A" Company, it appeared, had found themselves clinging grimly to the section of Fosse Alley which they had captured, with their left flank entirely in the air. Presently came an order. Farther forward still, half-right, another isolated trench was being held by a portion of the Highland Brigade. These were suffering cruelly, for the German artillery had the range to a nicety, and convenient sap-heads gave the German bombers easy access to the flanks. It is more than likely that this very trench had been constructed expressly for the inveiglement of a too successful attacking party. Certainly no troops could live in it for long. "A" Company were to go forward and support.

Captain Blaikie, passing word to his men to be ready, turned to Bobby.

"I'm a morose, dour, monosyllabic Scot, Bobbie," he said; "but this sort of thing bucks me up."

Next moment he was over the parapet and away, followed by his Company. In that long, steadily-advancing line were many of our friends. Muckle-wame was there, panting heavily, and cannily commending his soul to Providence. Messrs Ogg and Hogg were there, shoulder to shoulder. McOstrich, the Ulster visionary, was there, six paces ahead of any other man, crooning some Ironside canticle to himself. Next behind him came the reformed revolutionary, McSlattery.

Straightway the enemy observed the oncoming reinforcements, and shrapnel began to fly. The men pressed on, at a steady double now. McOstrich was the first to go down. Game to the last, he waved encouragement to his mates with a failing arm as they passed over his body.

"Come along, boys!" cried Captain Blaikie, suddenly eloquent. "There is the trench! The other lads are waiting for you. Come along! Charge!"

The men needed no further bidding. They came on — with a ragged cheer — and assuredly would have arrived, but for one thing. Suddenly they faltered, and stopped dead.

Captain Blaikie turned to his faithful subaltern panting behind him.

"We are done in, Bobby," he said. "Look! Wire!"

He was right. This particular trench, it was true, was occupied by our friends; but it had been constructed in the first instance for the use of our enemies. Consequently it was wired, and heavily wired, upon the side facing the British advance.

Captain Blaikie, directing operations with a walking-stick as if the whole affair were an Aldershot field-day, signalled to the Company to lie down, and began to unbutton a leather pouch in his belt.

"You too, Bobby," he said; "and don't dare to move a muscle until you get the order!"

He strolled forward, pliers in hand, and began methodically to cut a passage, strand by strand, through the forest of wire.

Then it was that invisible machine-guns opened, and a very gallant officer and Scotsman fell dead upon the field of honour.

Half an hour later, "A" Company, having expended all their ammunition and gained never a yard, fell back upon the rest of the Battalion. Including Bobby Little (who seemed to bear a charmed life), they did not represent the strength of a platoon.

"I wonder what they will do with us next," remarked Mr Waddell, who had finished his bully.

"If they have any sense of decency," said Major Kemp, "they will send us back to rest a bit, and put another Division in. We have opened the ball and done a lot of dirty work for them, and have lost a lot of men and officers. Bed for me, please!"

"I should be more inclined to agree with you, Major," said Wagstaffe, "if only we had a bit more to show for our losses."

"We haven't done so badly," replied Kemp, who was growing more cheerful under the influence of hot cocoa. "We have got the Hohenzollern, and the Boche first line at least, and probably Fosse Eight. On the right I hear we have taken Loos. That's not so dusty for a start. I have not the slightest doubt that there will be a heavy counter-attack, which we shall repel. After that we shall attack again, and gain more ground, or at least keep the Boche exceedingly busy holding on. That is our allotted task in this entertainment: to go on hammering the Hun, occupying his attention and using up his reserves regardless of whether we gain ground or lose it, while our French pals on the right are pushing him off the map. At least, that is my theory: I don't pretend to be in touch with the official mind. This battle will probably go on for a week or more, over practically the same ground. It will be dreadful for the wounded, but even if we only hold on to what we have gained already, we are the winners. Still, I wish we could have consolidated Fosse Alley before going to bed."

At this moment the Colonel, stooping low in the tiny doorway, entered the dug-out, followed by the Adjutant. He bade his supporters good morning.

"I am glad to find that you fellows have been able to give your men a meal," he said. "It was capital work getting the ration-carts up so far last night."

"Any news, Colonel?" asked Major Kemp.

"Most decidedly. It seems that the enemy have evacuated Fosse Alley again. Nobody quite knows why: a sudden attack of cold feet, probably. Our people command their position from Fosse Eight, on their left rear, so I don't altogether blame them. Whoever holds Fosse Eight holds Fosse Alley. However, the long and short of it all is that the Brigade are to go forward again this evening, and reoccupy Fosse Alley. Meanwhile, we consolidate things here."

Major Kemp sighed.

"Bed indefinitely postponed!" he remarked resignedly.

*　　*　　*　　*

By midnight on the same Sunday the Battalion, now far under its original strength, had re-entered the scene of yesterday's long struggle, filing thither under the stars, by a deserted and ghostly German *boyau* nearly ten feet deep. Fosse Alley erred in the opposite direction. It was not much more than four feet in depth; the chalky parapet could by no stretch of imagination be described as bullet-proof; dug-outs and communication trenches were non-existent. On our left the trench-line was continued by the troops of another Division: on our right lay another battalion of our own brigade.

"If the line has been made really continuous this time," observed the Colonel, "we should be as safe as houses. Wonderful fellows, these sappers! They have wired almost our whole front already. I wish they had had time to do it on our left as well."

Within the next few hours all defensive preparations possible in the time had been completed; and our attendant angels, most effectively disguised as Royal Engineers, had flitted away, leaving us to wait for Monday morning — and Brother Boche.

With the dawn, our eyes, which had known no sleep since Friday night, peered rheumily out over the whitening landscape.

To our front the ground stretched smooth and level for two hundred yards, then fell gently away, leaving a clearly defined skyline. Beyond the skyline rose houses, of which we could descry only the roofs and upper windows.

"That must be either Haisnes or Douvrin," said Major Kemp. "We are much farther to the left than we were yesterday. By the way, *was* it yesterday?"

"The day before yesterday, sir," the ever-ready Waddell informed him.

"Never mind; today's the day, anyhow. And it's going to be a busy day, too. The fact is, we are in a tight place, and all through doing too well. We have again penetrated so much farther forward than anyone else in our neighbourhood that we *may* have to fall back a bit. But I hope not. We have a big stake, Waddell. If we can hold on to this position until the others make good upon our right and left, we shall have reclaimed a clear two miles of the soil of France, my son." The Major swept the horizon with his glasses. "Let me see: that is probably Hulluch away on our right front: the Loos towers must be in line with us on our extreme right, but we can't see them for those hillocks. There is our old friend Fosse Eight towering over us on our left rear. I don't know anything about the ground on our absolute left, but so long as that flat-head regiment hold on to their trench, we can't go far wrong. Waddell, I don't like those cottages on our left front. They block the view, and also spell machine-guns. I see one or two very suggestive loopholes in those red-tiled roofs. Go and draw Ayling's attention to them. A little preliminary *strafeing* will do them no harm."

Five minutes later one of Ayling's machine-guns spoke out, and a cascade of tiles came sliding down the roofs of the offending cottages.

"That will tickle them up, if they have any guns set up on those rafters," observed the Major, with ghoulish satisfaction. "I wonder if Brer Boche is going to attack. I hope he does. There is only one thing I am afraid of, and that is that there may be some odd saps running out towards us, especially on our flanks. If so, we shall have some close work with bombs — a most ungentlemanly method of warfare. Let us pray for a straightforward frontal attack."

But Brer Boche had other cards to play first. Suddenly, out of nowhere, the air was filled with "whizz-bang" shells, moving in a lightning procession which lasted nearly half an hour. Most of these plastered the already scarred countenance of Fosse Eight: others fell shorter and demolished our parapet. When the tempest ceased, as suddenly as it began, the number of casualties in the crowded trench was considerable. But there was little time to attend to the wounded. Already the word was running down the line —

"Look out to your front!"

Sure enough, over the skyline, two hundred yards away, grey figures were appearing — not in battalions, but tentatively, in twos and threes. Next moment a storm of rapid rifle fire broke from the trench. The grey figures turned and ran. Some disappeared over the horizon, others dropped flat, others simply curled up and withered. In three minutes solitude reigned again, and the firing ceased.

"Well, that's that!" observed Captain Wagstaffe to Bobby Little, upon the right of the Battalion line. "The Boche has 'bethought himself and went,' as the poet says. Now he knows we are here, and have brought our arquebuses with us. He will try something more ikey next time. Talking of time, what about breakfast? When was our last meal, Bobby?"

"Haven't the vaguest notion," said Bobby sleepily.

"Well, it's about breakfast-time now. Have a bit of chocolate? It is all I have."

It was eight o'clock, and perfect silence reigned. All down the line men, infinitely grubby, were producing still grubbier fragments of bully-beef and biscuits from their persons. For an hour, squatting upon the sodden floor of the trench — it was raining yet again — the unappetising, intermittent meal proceeded.

Then —

"Hallo!" exclaimed Bobby with a jerk (for he was beginning to nod), "what was that on our right?"

"I'm afraid," replied Wagstaffe, "that it was bombs. It was right in this trench, too, about a hundred yards along. There must be a sap leading up there, for the bombers certainly have not advanced overground. I have been looking out for them since stand-to. Who is this anxious gentleman?"

A subaltern of the battalion on our right was forcing his way along the trench. He addressed Wagstaffe.

"We are having a pretty bad time with Boche bombers on our right, sir," he said. "Will you send us down all the bombs you can spare?"

Wagstaffe hoisted himself upon the parapet.

"I will see our C.O. at once," he replied, and departed at the double. It was a risky proceeding, for German bullets promptly appeared in close attendance; but he saved a good five minutes on his journey to Battalion Headquarters at the other end of the trench.

Presently the bombs began to arrive, passed from hand to hand. Wagstaffe returned, this time along the trench.

"We shall have a tough fight for it," he said. "The Boche bombers know their business, and probably have more bombs than we have. But those boys on our right seem to be keeping their end up."

"Can't *we* do anything?" asked Bobby feverishly.

"Nothing — unless the enemy succeed in working right down here; in which case we shall take our turn of getting it in the neck — or giving it! I fancy old Ayling and his pop-gun will have a word to say, if he can find a nice straight bit of trench. All we can do for the present is to keep a sharp look-out in front. I have no doubt they will attack in force when the right moment comes."

For close on three hours the bomb-fight went on. Little could be seen, for the struggle was all taking place upon the extreme right; but the sounds of conflict were plain enough. More bombs were passed up, and yet more; men, some cruelly torn, were passed down.

Then a signal-sergeant doubled up across country from somewhere in rear, paying out wire, and presently the word went forth that we were in touch with the Artillery. Directly after, sure enough, came the blessed sound and sight of British shrapnel bursting over our right front.

"That won't stop the present crowd," said Wagstaffe, "but it may prevent their reinforcements from coming up. We are holding our own, Bobby. What's that, Sergeant?"

"The Commanding Officer, sirr," announced Sergeant Carfrae, "has just passed up that we are to keep a sharp look-out to our left. They've commenced for to bomb the English regiment now."

"Golly, both flanks! This is getting a trifle steep," remarked Wagstaffe.

Detonations could now be distinctly heard upon the left.

"If they succeed in getting round behind us," said Wagstaffe in a low voice to Bobby, "we shall have to fall back a bit, into line with the rest of the advance. Only a few hundred yards, but it means a lot to *us!*"

"It hasn't happened yet," said Bobby stoutly.

Captain Wagstaffe knew better. His more experienced eye and ear had detected the fact that the position of the regiment upon the left was already turned. But he said nothing.

Presently the tall figure of the Colonel was seen, advancing in leisurely fashion along the trench, stopping here and there to exchange a word with a private or a sergeant.

"The regiment on the left may have to fall back, men," he was saying. "We, of course, will stand fast, and cover their retirement."

This most characteristic announcement was received with a matter-of-fact "Varra good, sir," from its recipients, and the Colonel passed on to where the two officers were standing.

"Hallo, Wagstaffe," he said; "good morning! We shall get some very pretty shooting practice presently.

The enemy are massing on our left front, down behind those cottages. How are things going on our right?"

"They are holding their own, sir,"

"Good! Just tell Ayling to get his guns trained. But doubtless he has done so already. I must get back to the other flank."

And back to the danger-spot our C.O. passed — an upright, gallant figure, saying little, exhorting not at all, but instilling confidence and cheerfulness by his very presence.

Half-way along the trench he encountered Major Kemp.

"How are things on the left, sir?" was the Major's *sotto voce* inquiry.

"Not too good. Our position is turned. We have been promised reinforcements, but I doubt if they can get up in time. Of course, when it comes to falling back, this regiment goes last."

"Of course, sir."

*   *   *   *

Highlanders! Four hundred yards! At the enemy advancing half-left, rapid fire!

Twenty minutes had passed. The regiment still stood immovable, though its left flank was now utterly exposed. All eyes and rifles were fixed upon the cluster of cottages. Through the gaps that lay between these could be discerned the advance of the German infantry — line upon line, moving towards the trench upon our left. The ground to our front was clear. Each time one of these lines passed a gap the rifles rang out and Ayling's remaining machine-gun uttered joyous barks. Still the enemy advanced. His shrapnel was bursting overhead; bullets were whistling from nowhere, for the attack in force was now being pressed home in earnest.

The deserted trench upon our left ran right through

the cottages, and this restricted our view. No hostile bombers could be seen; it was evident that they had done their bit and handed on the conduct of affairs to others. Behind the shelter of the cottages the infantry were making a safe detour, and were bound, unless something unexpected happened, to get round behind us.

"They'll be firing from our rear in a minute," said Kemp between his teeth. "Lochgair, order your platoon to face about and be ready to fire over the parados."

Young Lochgair's method of executing this command was characteristically thorough. He climbed in leisurely fashion upon the parados; and standing there, with all his six-foot-three in full view, issued his orders.

"Face this way, boys! Keep your eyes on that group of buildings just behind the empty trench, in below the Fosse. You'll get some target practice presently. Don't go and forget that you are the straightest-shooting platoon in the Company. There they are" — he pointed with his stick — "lots of them — coming through that gap in the wall! Now then, rapid fire, and let them have it! Oh, well done, boys! Good shooting! Very good! Very good ind —"

He stopped suddenly, swayed and toppled back into the trench. Major Kemp caught him in his arms, and laid him gently down upon the chalky floor. There was nothing more to be done. Young Lochgair had given his platoon their target, and the platoon were now firing steadily upon the same. He closed his eyes and sighed, like a tired child.

"Carry on, Major!" he murmured faintly. "I'm all right."

So died the simple-hearted, valiant enthusiast whom we had christened Othello.

The entire regiment — what was left of it — was now

firing over the back of the trench; for the wily Teuton had risked no frontal attack, seeing that he could gain all his ends from the left flank. Despite vigorous rifle fire and the continuous maledictions of the machine-gun, the enemy were now pouring through the cottages behind the trench. Many grey figures began to climb up the face of Fosse Eight, where apparently there was none to say them nay.

"We shall have a cheery walk back, I *don't* think!" murmured Wagstaffe.

He was right. Presently a withering fire was opened from the summit of the Fosse, which soon began to take effect in the exiguous and ill-protected trench.

"The Colonel is wounded, sir," reported the Sergeant-Major to Major Kemp.

"Badly?"

"Yes, sir."

Kemp looked round him. The regiment was now alone in the trench, for the gallant company upon their right had been battered almost out of existence.

"We can do no more good by staying here any longer," said the Major. "We have done our little bit. I think it is a case of 'Home, John!' Tell off a party to bring in the C.O., Sergeant-Major."

Then he passed the order.

"Highlanders, retire to the trenches behind, by companies, beginning from the right."

"Whatever we may think of the Boche as a gentleman," mused that indomitable philosopher, Captain Wagstaffe, as he doubled stolidly rearward behind his Company, "there is no denying his bravery as a soldier or his skill in co-ordinating an attack. It's positively uncanny, the way his artillery supports his infantry. (Hallo, that was a near one!) This enfilade fire from the Fosse is most unpleasant. (I fancy that one went through my kilt.) Steady there, on the left: don't bunch, whatever you do! Thank heaven, there's the next line of trenches, fully manned. And thank God, there's that boy Bobby tumbling in unhurt!"

*   *   *   *

So ended our share in the Big Push. It was a very small episode, spread over quite a short period, in one of the biggest and longest battles in the history of the world. It would have been easy to select a more showy episode, but hard to find a better illustration of the character of the men who took part in it. The battle which began upon that grey September morning has been raging, as I write, for nearly three weeks. It still surges backwards and forwards over the same stricken mile of ground; and the end is not yet. But the Hun is being steadily beaten to earth. (Only yesterday, in one brief furious counter-attack, he lost eight thousand killed.) When the final advance comes, as come it must, and our victorious line sweeps forward, it will pass over two narrow, ill-constructed, shell-torn trenches. In and around those trenches will be found the earthly remains of men — Jocks and Jimmies, and Sandies and Andies — clad in the uniform of almost every Scottish regiment. That assemblage of mute, glorious witnesses marks the point reached, during the first few hours of the first day's fighting, by the Scottish Division of "K(1)". *Molliter ossa cubent.*

There is little more to add to the record of those three days. For yet another night we carried on — repelling counter-attacks, securing the Hohenzollern, making sorties out of Big Willie, or manning the original front-line parapet against eventualities. As is inevitable in a fight of these proportions, whole brigades were mingled together, and unexpected leaders arose to take the place of those who had fallen. Many a stout piece of work was done that night by mixed bands of kilties, flat-heads, and even cyclists, marshalled in a captured German trench and shepherded by a junior subaltern.

Finally, about midnight, came the blessed order that fresh troops were coming up to continue the attack, and that we were to be extricated from the *mêlée* and sent back to rest. And so, after a participation in the battle of some seventy-two hours, our battered Division came out — to sleep the sleep of utter exhaustion in dug-outs behind the railway line, and to receive, upon waking, the thanks of its Corps Commander.

*   *   *   *

And here I propose (for a time, at least) to take leave of The First Hundred Thousand. Some day, if Providence wills, the tale shall be resumed; and you shall hear how Major Kemp, Captain Wagstaffe, Ayling and Bobby Little, assisted by such veterans as Corporal Mucklewame, built up the regiment, with copious drafts and a fresh batch of subalterns, to its former strength.

But the title of the story will have to be changed. In the hearts of those who drilled them, reasoned with them, sometimes almost wept over them, and ultimately fought shoulder to shoulder with them, the sturdy, valiant legions, whose humorously-pathetic career you have followed so patiently for fifteen months, will always be First; but, alas! they are no longer The Hundred Thousand.

So we will leave them, as is most justly due, in sole possession of their proud title.